"Here Dolores Curran has offered us a gentle, usable guide for teaching normal, everyday families to pray. For a generation of parents who may have grown up never learning the traditional prayers of the church, this book will be invaluable. For all families, the simple suggestions and uncomplicated rituals will foster both a sense of family unity and a deeper understanding of faith and the church year that celebrates it. The combination of beautiful prayers and unthreatening ideas reveal the soul of a woman whose passionate love of her family is matched only by her passionate love of God.

Kathleen O. Chesto
Author, *Family Prayer for Family Times*

"Dolores does it again—her revised book of family prayer is practical, readable, realistic, and inspiring. For families wanting to start or renew their life of prayer, she offers the basics in an easy-to-follow format. As always, she emphasizes that no family is perfect, but that every family can try and adapt these rituals and prayers.

"Her guidance has the authority of one who's been there—she has field tested these ideas with her own family. My only regret? I wish my kids were younger, and we could start all over again, having this book in hand!"

Kathy Coffey
Author, *Experiencing God with Your Children*

"Books on prayer abound, thank God. We certainly need them. But some are so solemn that it becomes a downright chore to get through them. Not so with Dolores Curran. Open this book to any page of its nine chapters and you will be 'hooked'.

"As a mother and educator Dolores shares with us her own experience of the spontaneity and joy that can spark prayer. This book will help us all to discover how praying can be a delightful expression of love—God's for us and ours for God."

Sr. Maria de la Cruz Aymes, S.H.
San Francisco, CA

"Lucky the kids who grow up in a family climate cultivated by the faith practices encouraged in this book! What fun! What drama! What overcoming of boredom! Nothing is forced, and no one need feel left out. Everyone has a role. Every family would love to have such a design for prayer. For example, how could lenten prayers be so original, so dramatic? That alone is one factor to recommend this book highly. And lucky the parents who use this imaginative and practical guide."

Mary Luke Tobin, S.L.
Thomas Merton Center for Creative Exchange
Denver, CO

"I found Dolores Curran's revised book on family prayer a very helpful and uncomplicated resource for parents who are looking for ideas to foster family prayer. It has great variety, in that it includes all the traditional prayers of our Catholic faith as well as many new and creative ways to introduce children and families to newer forms of prayer.

"I think it will be a great help to any parent who wishes to make family prayer an important and vital part of family life, and it will help parents to introduce themselves and their children to a variety of forms of prayer and ways to observe family events and the feasts of the church year."

Fr. Tom Kramer
Cathedral of the Holy Spirit
Bismarck, ND

DOLORES CURRAN

on

Family Prayer

TWENTY-THIRD PUBLICATIONS

Mystic, CT 06355

Revised and expanded 1997

Twenty-Third Publications
185 Willow Street
P.O. Box 180
Mystic, CT 06355
(860) 536-2611
800-321-0411

ISBN 0-89622-703-0
Library of Congress Catalog Card Number 96-60656
Printed in the U.S.A.

CONTENTS

Dolores Curran on Family Prayer

A Parent's Prayer

God, you sent these children to us
and you sent us to them.
Only you know why.

But we're doing the best we can
with what you sent...
and so are they.

Lord, help us all.

Amen.

INTRODUCTION

"So you're Dolores Curran," a young father said, eyeing me speculatively before a workshop. "My mother raised me on you."

We both laughed and he went on to relate some of the traditions and rituals initiated by his mother after she read the original edition of *Family Prayer* in the late seventies. "When we were early teenagers and she would suggest something new, we would groan and say, 'Have you been reading Dolores Curran again?'"

As I slide into my sixties I am heartened by comments like his because these young parents are present in workshops and classes on family spirituality. Their childhood faith experiences didn't damage them or turn them off to God or church. Their very presence tells us that in spite of their moans, groans, and sometimes downright sabotage at the time, something valuable in family faith experiences took root which they want to pass on to their own children.

That's why I'm revising and offering this little book to a new generation of parents. When I wrote it in 1978, my children, now adults, were still young and I was struggling with what then seemed like major issues: messy rooms, sassy mouths, and occasional notes from the teacher. But God got us through those years with prayer, humility, and a lot of humor.

I went on to other books and, like most books, *Family Prayer* eventually went out of print. I forgot about it. Then, in the space of a month, it cropped up three times. I received a call from a woman asking for copies for her married children and she expressed intense disappointment when I couldn't furnish them. "I raised my kids on that book and they want to do the same," she said. "Is there any place I can find it?" I was unable to help her.

A week later in Madison, Wisconsin, where I was addressing a large group of family life ministers, the staff laid out a display of my past books from their family resource library. Several attendees tried to buy *Family Prayer* out of the display. When told it was not for sale and out of print, one wailed, "Where are the books we need when we need them?" I smiled in empathy and promptly dismissed the incident.

But when I returned home, there was a letter from Neil Kluepfel of Twenty-Third Publications, the original publisher of the book, asking me to consider revising it for reissue. "There's a new generation of parents out there looking for material like this," he said. And, because he added some nice words about the book and me, I agreed. Slow learner that I am, I finally figured God was nudging me into revising this book. It's an interesting experience—a little like getting a second chance to rear the same child, only this time, maybe getting it right.

Originally, I wrote *Family Prayer* in response to requests from parents in my parenting classes for some easy, comfortable religious traditions and rituals that fit the busy lifestyle of families twenty years ago. If anything, that lifestyle has become even busier, and today's parents have an even greater need than those of twenty years ago for ideas and encouragement on comfortably inviting God into the family circle.

In spite of the grim statistics and stories about the demise of the family—a demise that has been direly predicted since Cain slew Abel—hundreds of thousands of ordinary families exist, families who hunger for meaning beyond power, prestige, and possessions. They want to be strong families but they don't always know how.

Sometimes they long for past eras that are more nostalgic than accurate in media portrayals. As a cynic quipped, "Nostalgia consists of idealizing the past we don't want to return to."

But the appeal of these idyllic representations of family life of yore manifests two yearnings of modern families: they long for a simpler lifestyle and for a life with meaning. When they watch reruns of the Waltons gathered around the hearth singing, they wonder if and how they can reproduce the experience in their own homes, surrounded as they are by television, telephone, computer games, and videos which usurp the hearth and communication. When they view the family of Anne Frank celebrating a joyous Hanukkah in the midst of the Holocaust, they wonder how we lost the traditions and rituals that give richness and strength to families in times of trials.

Thomas Merton wrote, "All we need is to experience what we already possess." Most families do not recognize that they already possess that elusive meaning which they seek. They have within themselves the resources and strengths of the Walton and Frank families. Like Anne Frank, their children are waiting for their parents to take action, to proclaim, "Today is an important day in our lives because...."

Family prayer isn't always going to be what we would like it to be. Sometimes it's going to be strained, sometimes downright awful. I have worked with many families in many denominations and recognize the same fears, uncertainties, and hopes. Many fear they have waited too long, that because their oldest children are in adolescence, it's too late to start. Then, with despair, they see their adolescents drawn to families, groups, and movements which fill the spiritual hunger missing in their own family life, missing because their parents are too timid or too busy to feed it.

Other parents fear they are starting too early or pushing too hard. These fears can be overcome when parents share one desire in common—a desire for a richer spiritual bonding in the family. They are willing to try and fail, turning their feeble attempts over to God with humility and humor.

But, oh, those glorious moments in family life when whatever we're doing works, when we actually experience God in our midst, make it all worthwhile. These are the sacred moments that indicate and prove to families what they can truly become, the moments Pope John Paul II described in his poignant plea to families, "Family, become what you are...a community of life and love" (§17, *Familiaris Consortio*, 1981).

Let's become a community of love, of faith, of the richness that already exists within us. Let's allow the rituals, feelings, and prayers to emerge and flourish. If our children experience them with us in our families, they need not seek them elsewhere.

One father, initially reluctant to go along with his wife's idea of implementing some simple spiritual traditions in their family, became a great supporter when he experienced the bonding and love that's allowed to emerge during these times. "Maybe we aren't doing anything productive," he mused, "but at least we're making memories for our children."

Making memories is what family life is all about. When my now-grownup children start reminiscing about their childhood, they don't talk about the Little League games they played or the four-basic-food-group meals I dished up, or the report card hassles we endured. They talk about the sharing times, the silly times, those special times of decorating Easter eggs and Christmas cookies, sitting around the Christmas tree in a darkened room, and listening to stories in the car.

To quote Merton again, "The church and the world do not need people to talk about prayer, think about prayer, or write about prayer nearly as much as they need people to pray."

So, I feel a little guilty writing about prayer instead of praying. But I do pray and hope that families will use this book as a spark and a resource, not a substitute for prayer. I offer this book which comes from the richness of the many families with whom I've worked. Like mine, they aren't perfect families but they are real families. It is in their reality that we are blessed.

I invite families to take from these pages whatever will help them to become what they already are, because all families deserve to be communities of love.

TEACHING
TRADITIONAL
PRAYERS

"Do memorized prayers have any value?" parents often ask. "I don't see the point in teaching them if children don't understand what they're saying."

Yes, memorized prayers do have value, as long as they are not the only prayers offered a child. The primary value of memorizing any material, whether it's prayers with incomprehensible words, history dates, or math tables, is that the material is there when the person grows up to understand and need it. Maybe children won't understand all the words in a prayer now, but later on, when they are in need of a quick reassuring prayer, they will reach for it and understand it. And it will be there because they learned it.

One caution: parents should not teach the more complex prayers too soon, but rather begin with the simple, understandable ones.

The first prayer I remember learning as a child was "Angel of God," or the Guardian Angel prayer. I can still conjure up my very own angel who sat at the foot of my bed and watched over me once the lights went out. It is an immensely reassuring prayer when you are little and frightened of being alone or of things that go bump in the night.

When I became a parent and experienced my children's fears, I came to realize even more the value of a personal guardian angel and the prayer that goes with it. Contrast this with the line in the classic children's prayer, "If I should die before I wake." What a horrible prayer to say with children at bedtime! I would never teach my children a prayer that instilled fear.

For a toddler's first prayer, I don't think this one can be surpassed:

Guardian Angel Prayer
Angel of God, my guardian dear, to whom God's love commits me here, ever this day, be at my side, to light and guard, to rule and guide. Amen.

Mastering the Basics
It was always an occasion in my childhood family when the youngest mastered the Sign of the Cross. Since there were seven of us close together, the young learner had a great deal of help—probably too much at times. I remember all of us watching and holding our breath when the toddler finally put the correct words with the correct motions at family mealtime. And that's how we taught the familiar basic prayers to our own children, by saying them as grace until they mastered them. This gives them practice, as well as a bit of glory and affirmation by loved ones.

Sign of the Cross
In the name of the Father, and of the Son, and of the Holy Spirit. Amen.

We like to follow the Sign of the Cross with the "Glory Be" which, incidentally, makes a fine prayer to end the family meal. Simply bow your heads together and say:

Doxology
Glory be to the Father, and to the Son, and to the Holy Spirit, as it was in the beginning, is now, and ever shall be, world without end. Amen.

We taught our children the Our Father and the Hail Mary in bits and pieces so they could better understand and assimilate each phrase. At mealtime, we began with "Our Father, who art in heaven" and talked a little about that word *art*. Since most children run into poetic and archaic language only in prayers, it's important to let them know that words like *art, thou,* and *thy* are retained because of tradition, much like the *'twas* in "'Twas the night before Christmas." Otherwise, as they grow up they will tend to equate outdated language with outdated prayer.

At mealtime or bedtime try teaching the Our Father in several segments rather than one large gulp. Here's how we did it:

Monday: "'Our Father, who art in heaven.' Let's all say it together a few times. Good! Tomorrow night we'll see if we can remember it and, if we do, we'll add the next line."

Tuesday: "Who remembers the first line to the Our Father? Good, let's hear you say it. That was fine, Tim. Oh, you remember it too, Sue? Good. Anybody else? Okay, the next line is 'Hallowed be thy name.' Let's say it together. Good. Does anyone know which two words are said exactly the way they were hundreds of years ago? Right: *hallowed* and *thy*. Want to guess what they mean?"

Wednesday: "Let's say the first two lines together: 'Our Father, who art in heaven, hallowed be thy name.' Good.

Let's try it again. Okay, now we add 'Thy kingdom come, thy will be done.'" And so on....

This is a better approach than simply having a child memorize a lot of words like a television commercial. It also shows that the prayer is important enough for the family to talk about, not just learn.

The Lord's Prayer

Our Father, who art in heaven, hallowed be thy name; thy kingdom come; thy will be done on earth as it is in heaven. Give us this day our daily bread; and forgive us our trespasses as we forgive those who trespass against us; and lead us not into temptation, but deliver us from evil. For thine is the kingdom and the power and the glory forever and ever. Amen.

Once your family has mastered the Our Father, go on to the Hail Mary. In both prayers there are some phrases and ideas that are too abstract for little minds, for example, "thy will be done" and "fruit of thy womb." Don't avoid them, but don't dwell on them either. Give the children the words so that, as they grow to understand, they can put the meaning to the words.

You might explain to a four-year-old, that "thy will be done" means that whatever God wants, you will do, or that "fruit of thy womb" means baby. Expect the child to ask, "Then how come we don't say it that way?" Be ready with your response: "Because it is a prayer that is hundreds of years old and it is nice to keep the language that way if you're big enough to be able to say it." The inference of maturity usually insures quick learning.

Hail Mary

Hail Mary, full of grace, the Lord is with thee. Blessed art thou among women and blessed is the fruit of thy womb,

Jesus. Holy Mary, mother of God, pray for us sinners, now and at the hour of our death. Amen.

"Thou" or "You"?

Another word here about language. Many parishes and teachers are using modern language in the standard prayers. There's nothing wrong with that. We attended a rosary service recently with relatives from many parts of the country and the responses were evenly divided between "the Lord is with thee" and "the Lord is with you." If you prefer to teach your children these modern versions of the old prayers, here they are:

Modern Lord's Prayer

Our Father in heaven, hallowed be your name. Your kingdom come; your will be done on earth as it is in heaven. Give us this day our daily bread; and forgive us our trespasses as we forgive those of others. Lead us not into temptation but deliver us from evil. For yours is the kingdom, the power, and the glory, now and forever. Amen.

Modern Hail Mary

Hail Mary, full of grace, the Lord is with you. Blessed are you among women and blessed is the fruit of your womb, Jesus. Holy Mary, Mother of God, pray for us sinners, now and at the hour of our death. Amen.

Grace

Although we much prefer spontaneous grace to the familiar "Bless us, O Lord," we feel it's important to teach our children the traditional Catholic grace. There are many times when it is used in large groups and in other homes and then they need the words.

Prayer Before Meals
Bless us, O Lord, and these your gifts which we are about
to receive from your bounty, through Christ, our Lord.
Amen.

The grace after meals is not said as often as it might be in
families. It just might be the right closing ritual between dessert
and the rush to turn on television.

Prayer After Meals
We give you thanks, Almighty God, for these and all your
blessings; you live and reign forever and ever. Amen.

Moving On
It's easy to teach our children to pray to God and to Jesus
because they are "people" to them. It's much harder to teach
them to pray to the Holy Spirit. I've found the best way with
small children is not to teach about the dove and the tongue of
fire which, because of their concrete level of understanding,
only confuses them more. Rather, you can teach that the Holy
Spirit is that feeling of love that emanates from God and Jesus,
much like the feeling of love children feel within the family. To
build up a devotion, it is necessary that a child hear about the
Holy Spirit. This traditional prayer said daily by the family helps
build familiarity:

Come, Holy Spirit
Come, Holy Spirit, fill the hearts of your faithful
    and kindle in them the fire of your love.
Send forth your Spirit and they shall be created
    and you will renew the face of the earth.
O God, you teach the hearts of the faithful
    by giving them the light of the Holy Spirit.

Grant that, in the same Spirit,
    we may be truly wise
    and ever rejoice in his consolation.
Through Christ, our Lord. Amen.

Once upon a church, we taught the Act of Contrition at age seven so that children could recite it at their first confession. Today various forms are used in the sacrament of reconciliation and it is possible that a Catholic would never "need" the Act of Contrition. But it is a traditional prayer that is both beautiful and meaningful. We taught it to our children when each turned ten years old, and used it during our family reconciliation rituals.

Act of Contrition
O my God, I am heartily sorry for having offended you, and I detest all my sins because of your just punishments, but most of all because they offend you, my God, who are all good and deserving of all my love. I firmly resolve, with the help of your grace, to sin no more and to avoid the near occasions of sin. Amen.

The Apostles' Creed is taught and used primarily for praying the rosary. It is traditionally the Creed that was encouraged for personal prayer, while the Nicene Creed, the one that we recite at Mass, was for liturgical use. Yet there's a problem today in teaching the Apostles' Creed to our children that we didn't face in the days before Vatican II. When the liturgy was commonly said in Latin, the Nicene Creed was recited in Latin, so we didn't confuse the two Creeds. But the Nicene Creed and the Apostles' Creed are just different enough to cause a good deal of confusion.

In our home, we didn't insist that our children learn both. One of our children did; the other two used the Creed from the Mass when we said the rosary.

Apostles' Creed

I believe in God, the Father Almighty, Creator of heaven and earth, and in Jesus Christ, his only Son, our Lord, who was conceived by the Holy Spirit, born of the Virgin Mary, suffered under Pontius Pilate, was crucified, died and was buried. He descended into hell; the third day he arose again from the dead. He ascended into heaven, sits at the right hand of God, the Father Almighty; from thence he shall come to judge the living and the dead.

I believe in the Holy Spirit, the Holy Catholic Church, the communion of saints, the forgiveness of sins, the resurrection of the body, and life everlasting. Amen.

The Rosary

Every family has little traditions and rituals. Our family had a whole series of them when we traveled. One was to say a rosary in the car every morning when we traveled; often this coincided with the rising of the sun. At that time of day, everyone was still a bit subdued and a little hungry, and it was a fine time to put our day on the road in God's hands.

Many parents report that their children dislike the rosary because they find it meaningless and repetitious. Yet many of these same children grow up to embrace forms of meditation which are based on meaningless repetition!

We found that if we emphasized the mysteries of the rosary rather than the prayers, our children responded well. When they were young, we began by telling a little story explaining each mystery. As they grew older, they gave a short (one or two sentence) explanation of each mystery.

Families have the opportunity to relax unhurriedly in the car. You can keep distractions to a minimum (turn off the radio and the car phone!), and the movement of the the vehicle itself can have a lulling effect (did you ever get a crying child to sleep by taking him or her for a ride?). Maybe that's why the rosary worked so much better for us in the car than anywhere else. I encourage other parents to try it when they travel, even if it's only a one-day trip. The family can take turns saying the decades and rotate the joyful, sorrowful, and glorious mysteries on different days. Here are the mysteries and the stories we told to accompany them:

The Joyful Mysteries

First Joyful Mystery: The Annunciation
When Mary was just a young girl, an angel came and said to her, "Hail Mary, full of grace, the Lord is with you." He asked her if she would be willing to become the mother of Jesus, and Mary said yes. We call it the Annunciation because the Angel *announced* that Mary was chosen to be the mother of Jesus.

Second Joyful Mystery: The Visitation
When Mary was pregnant, she visited her cousin Elizabeth, who was much older than she but was also pregnant with Jesus' cousin, John the Baptist. When Mary and Elizabeth hugged each other, their babies leaped inside as if they were greeting each other. Later on, it was John the Baptist who prepared the way for Jesus by telling people he was coming.

Third Joyful Mystery: The Nativity
This is Christmas, the birth of the infant Jesus. You know the story well, but let's recall it for a moment. Remember that Joseph and Mary had to go to Bethlehem to register for the census and while they were there, Jesus was born. There was no room at the inn so he was born in the stable. Later he was visited by shepherds and wise men.

Fourth Joyful Mystery: The Presentation
This is a little like Christian baptism today. Each Jewish baby was taken to the Temple and *presented* to the rabbi there. It was during this time that the old man, Simeon, who had been promised by God that he wouldn't die until he saw the savior of his people, saw Jesus and said, "Now I am ready to die. I have seen him."

Fifth Joyful Mystery: The Finding in the Temple
When Mary, Joseph and Jesus had gone to Jerusalem with a large group of people for a special day, the women walked back together and so did the men. At suppertime, when families gathered together again, Jesus wasn't there. Mary had thought he was with Joseph, who had thought Jesus was with the women. They had to walk the long way back and they must have been worried.

But they found him in the Temple listening to the teachers. And he was only thirteen years old! When they asked him why he hadn't come with them, Jesus told them he had to be about his Father's business. This was one of the first signs Mary and Joseph had that Jesus would be leaving them someday to do God's work.

The Sorrowful Mysteries

First Sorrowful Mystery: The Agony in the Garden
After the Last Supper, Jesus told his friends, the apostles, that he wanted to go to the garden to pray. They went with him and he went in a little farther to pray alone. When he came back they were asleep, and that disappointed him because he knew he wouldn't be with them much longer. After a while the soldiers, led by Judas, came and took him away to be tried and killed.

Second Sorrowful Mystery: The Scourging
Even though Jesus hadn't hurt anyone or been tried by a court of law yet, the soldiers stripped his clothes away and beat him.

Third Sorrowful Mystery: The Crowning with Thorns
The soldiers were making fun of Jesus. Because he said he was a king, they made a crown for him out of thorns and stuck it on his head until his skin bled. Then they pretended to bow before him as their king.

Fourth Sorrowful Mystery: The Carrying of the Cross
Jesus had to carry his own cross through town and up the hill to Calvary. On the way he fell three times, met his mother and said a silent goodbye to her, and was made fun of by the people in the street. Finally, he made it to Calvary where he was nailed to the cross.

Fifth Sorrowful Mystery: The Crucifixion
Jesus died on the cross. It took three hours of great pain and sadness. He was crucified between two thieves. One asked his forgiveness and Jesus said to him, "This day you shall be with me in heaven." When he died, his body was taken down and laid in Mary's arms.

The Glorious Mysteries

First Glorious Mystery: The Resurrection
The morning that Jesus rose from the dead, which we call Easter, some of the women were coming to his tomb to anoint his body. When they got there, the stone was rolled back and an angel told them Jesus was gone. They ran into town to tell the men, who were hiding. There was

great rejoicing when they heard. Thomas, one of the followers, didn't believe. So Jesus came to them in the Upper Room and asked Thomas to put his hands on his wounds so he could believe it really was Jesus.

Second Glorious Mystery: The Ascension
After a while on earth, Jesus arranged to meet his disciples on a mountaintop and told them to continue his work. They remembered when he had told them that in a little while they would not see him but then in another while they would. He promised he would be with them always in new and wonderful ways. Then he rose into the heavens and disappeared into the clouds.

Third Glorious Mystery: The Descent of the Holy Spirit
After Jesus ascended into heaven, the apostles were gathered together praying when the Holy Spirit descended upon them. Suddenly they were filled with great love and knowledge. Every person listening to them could understand them, regardless of the language the listener spoke.

In our church today, we call this Pentecost Sunday. Some people call it the birthday of our church because it gave the apostles the courage and wisdom to go out and preach.

Fourth Glorious Mystery: The Assumption
We do not know how this happened but we do know that Mary died and went to heaven. We can just imagine what a glorious reunion there was between Mary and her son. She was *assumed*, or taken up body and soul, into heaven. That's why we call it the Assumption.

Fifth Glorious Mystery:
The Crowning of Mary as Queen of Heaven
Mary, as the mother of Jesus, reigns as queen in heaven.

Remember that, when Jesus was dying, he gave his mother to all of us. In heaven, she remains our mother and our queen. That is why we pray the rosary to her and speak to her in times of love and need.

More Mature Prayers

As children get older, they want more mature prayers. "Angel of God" seems too babyish to them (although they may whisper it in the dark), and some of the others are too mechanical. The family should constantly add new prayers to their repertoire so that praying becomes a growing rather than a stagnant tradition.

An old favorite of mine, the Morning Offering, seems foreign to many children and adults today. I offer it here to your family as a good way to face each day.

Morning Offering

O Jesus, through the Immaculate Heart of Mary, I offer you my prayers, works, joys, and sufferings of this day in union with the Holy Sacrifice of the Mass throughout the world. Amen.

I got through many a test, argument, and date with the aid of the Memorare. This beautiful prayer shouldn't be allowed to be forgotten. In May say it with your family during grace or include it in your Mary rituals.

Memorare

Remember, O most gracious Virgin Mary, that never was it known that anyone who fled to your protection, implored your help, or sought your intercession was left unaided. Inspired by this confidence, we fly unto you, O Virgin of virgins, our Mother!

To you we come, before you we stand, sinful and sor-

rowful. O Mother of the Word Incarnate, despise not our
petitions, but in your mercy hear and answer us. Amen.

In a survey taken of Catholics who experienced both the pre-
Vatican II and the post-Vatican II church, respondents reported
that more than anything else they missed Benediction, the ritual that used to end evening novenas, Stations of the Cross, and
missions in the pre-Vatican II church. Maybe it was the
grandeur and incense of this service, or maybe it was the combined ritual and language. (At that time, of course, the Mass and
even the Solemn Forty Hours were conducted in Latin, so we
weren't certain what was being said. But we always knew what
was taking place during Benediction.)

Benediction ended with the Divine Praises. I am including
them here, not because I think families should hold
Benediction at home, but because these might be useful in family celebrations and parents might thus be able to preserve them
for their children.

Divine Praises

Blessed be God.
Blessed be his Holy Name.
Blessed be Jesus Christ, true God and true Man.
Blessed be the name of Jesus.
Blessed be his most Sacred Heart.
Blessed be his most Precious Blood.
Blessed be Jesus in the most holy Sacrament of the Altar.
Blessed be the Holy Spirit, the Paraclete.
Blessed be the great Mother of God, Mary Most Holy.
Blessed be her Holy and Immaculate Conception.
Blessed be her Glorious Assumption.
Blessed be the name of Mary, Virgin and Mother.
Blessed be St. Joseph, her most chaste spouse.
Blessed be God in his angels and his saints.

Family Favorites

Finally, here is my favorite prayer, the Prayer of St. Francis of Assisi. It states the Christian apostolate so perfectly and in such beautiful language that I see it as a highly valuable prayer for the family, especially for young people. It has been put to music by several religious singers and groups; these beautiful songs can be used in family celebrations, especially during Advent, Lent, and reconciliation rituals.

Prayer of St. Francis of Assisi

Lord, make me an instrument of your peace.
Where there is hatred, let me sow love;
    where there is injury, pardon;
    where there is doubt, faith;
    where there is despair, hope;
    where there is darkness, light;
    and where there is sadness, joy.
O Divine Master, grant that I may not so much seek
    to be consoled as to console;
    to be understood, as to understand;
    to be loved, as to love.
For it is in giving that we receive,
    it is in pardoning that we are pardoned,
    and it is in dying that we are born to eternal life. Amen.

For those favorite prayers of your family that I have failed to put in this chapter, here are a few blank pages. By writing them in, you are personalizing this family collection of prayers and keeping them all together in one place.

YOUR FAMILY PRAYERS

YOUR FAMILY PRAYERS

YOUR FAMILY PRAYERS

2

PRAYING SPONTANEOUSLY

Hi again, God.
How are you today? I am fine.
One question I wonder about:
How come you don't fall out of heaven?
Well, that's all I've got to say, I guess.
Gotta go now. 'Bye.

—Prayer of nine-year-old Mark

Sometimes after I've given a talk on prayer and celebration in the family, a listener will object to the idea of spontaneous or natural prayer because it detracts from memorized prayers. I call this the "either/or" mentality. Why can't we have both? We say what we want to say to God.

I think it's sad when a child hasn't learned his or her prayers, but I think it is far sadder when a grownup can't pray spontaneously. One thing is obvious, though: The earlier the child is exposed to spontaneous prayer, the more comfortable the child will be with it.

When the child is very young, say the "Angel of God" as a bedtime ritual and then add a homemade prayer of your own such as:

Thank you, God, for Timmy and for this good day. Amen.
or:
Take care of us tonight, Jesus, and keep us well. Amen.
or:
Jesus, help us to love one another and you, tomorrow and every day. Amen.
or:
God bless Grandma, Grandpa, my friends....

Don't repeat the same thing every night, and encourage your child to add his or her own words. Be prepared for some strange prayers like, "And Jesus, please hit Danny for me because he took my Big Wheel." Spontaneous prayer is just that. If we land heavily on our children for praying in their own words to God, they will soon be praying in our words, and that defeats the idea.

Begin at Meals

Family grace is by far the most effective time to teach spontaneity in prayer. The dinner table is the only time many families get together in our hectic culture. If parents use it for intimacy with one another and God, it implants the idea that God is an integral part of family life.

Parents serve as models in teaching family grace. Get into the habit of saying something like this before meals:

O God, we thank you for this food, for the rain today which we need, for Tommy's field trip to the museum, and for each other. Amen.

That's enough for young children. Keep it simple, understandable, and short. If there are two parents, take turns saying
grace. The whole family responds with a simple "Amen."

When the oldest child is able, invite him or her to say a
homemade grace. You will be surprised at how comfortable
and capable your child will be after hearing and watching you
do it. The first grace is likely to be something like this:

> Jesus,
>> thanks for the chicken and the potatoes
>> and the milk and the peaches
>> and Grandma and today. Amen.

Sometimes you may have to cut your child off. Unused to
commanding such rapt attention, he or she may go on endlessly. Do it gently by saying, at a pause for breath, "...and thank
you, Jesus, for such a good grace. Amen."

You can also adopt the technique of having one of the parents say the grace and each of the children add a prayer of
thanks, like this:

Parent:	We thank you, God, for this family, for our home, for all our various works today, and for this good food.
Second Parent:	Thanks for helping me get all my work done today.
Oldest child:	Thanks for letting me catch the bus which I almost missed.
Second child:	Thank you, Jesus, for getting my paper put up on the bulletin board.

As children get up into third grade or older, they can take on
the family grace all by themselves. Many families tell me that
they like to alternate from oldest to youngest because this gives
the grace a freshness at each meal.

A word here about song: if your family is uncomfortable praying together in the beginning, try singing the "great Amen" or one of the familiar hymns from Sunday Mass as a grace. Add a thanks for the food, either before or after the song. This is an especially effective way of getting into natural prayer in a family where there is no tradition of it, or where there are preteens or teens. (Someone once observed that the songs of today are our youth's poetry. I think they are also their prayers, and that teenagers are often more comfortable singing their prayers than saying them.)

If the family is really uncomfortable about spontaneous prayer, try the old memorized "Bless us, O Lord" and add a phrase or two of thanks. Gradually increase this until you can drop the security of the memorized prayer in favor of original prayer. Don't rush it. It may take some time, particularly if your children are older and used to a five-second grace instead of a two-minute one. But keep in mind that you are taking the effort to furnish a balanced meal. Why not a balanced family—parents, children, and God?

Mealtime prayer also offers us the opportunity to *touch*. In many families today members do not touch one another in any loving way. They do not hug, kiss, or throw their arms about the shoulders, even after an absence from one another. Yet there is a great hunger for touch in both parents and children. If your family is disadvantaged in this way, try joining hands for family grace. It's a simple yet loving gesture that is nonthreatening to even the most closed off member of the family.

I once worked with a family that did everything "right" from scrupulous attendance at Mass, church meetings, and religious education to keeping a chart on the children's morning and night prayers; but this family had no sense of intimacy, no touching, no openness to one another.

The parents dutifully attended a lecture I gave in their parish about family prayer and celebration, and they came up afterward to ask me if it was too late to instill a sense of celebration and openness in their family's spiritual and emotional life. I suggested they continue with their spiritual "regimen" (that's how I viewed it!), but that they add one new ritual: before dinner they were to join hands and sing the "great Amen."

They reported back that it was awkward for the family at first, but before long they were able to drop the formal grace and get into spontaneous prayer and eventually some other family rituals. What struck me was the mother's comment, "You know, I think what we all like most is holding hands." In that family just the holding of hands was both a gift from and a prayer to God.

From Mealtime to the Rest of the Time

Once the family is comfortable with spontaneous prayer before meals, try expanding it to other times during the day. Again, you as parent are model.

How naturally you invoke God, Jesus, the Holy Spirit, Mary, and patron saints during the day is apt to be how your children will invoke them also. If you save prayer for those rare occasions when it's quiet and you have 15 minutes to get down on your knees privately, so will your children. If you are in the car and glimpse a view of the mountains and breathe a spontaneous, "Thanks, God, for such beautiful mountains," so will your child come to pair creation and thanksgiving. If an ambulance goes by and you say aloud, "Dear God, bless the person in that ambulance. Please keep that person from too much pain," your listening child will pair God's saving grace with your concern for others.

A natural time for such spontaneous prayer is the moment of waking a child in the morning. Say something like this as you touch the child's shoulders:

Good morning, Katie! Time to get up. Thanks, Lord, for my little Katie and for a brand new day.

Contrast that greeting with the more usual shout on your way to the kitchen, "Get up, Pete! It's seven o'clock."

Other natural times for spontaneous prayer are those moments during the day which call for a quick expression of praise, thanks, or need. When your son comes home from school crushed because he was the last one chosen in the recess ball game, the parent who is comfortable with prayer can say, "That's really too bad, Joe," then take the child's hand and say:

We know someone has to be last in everything, Jesus. Please help us to learn to be last sometimes. Still, it hurts to be last. Help Joe's hurt not to be so great.

This little prayer may not seem to be much on the surface, even schmaltzy, but let's look at its values. First, it brings God in on concrete matters in daily life. Second, it implants the idea in the child's mind that somebody has to be last. Third, it affords an opportunity for touching. And fourth, it tells the child that the parent understands and is on his side.

Joe will probably eat a banana or two and go out and find someone to play with; and the parent will have an hour or so before the next child comes home, say a junior-high-age daughter who has just made the gymnastics team. It's just as important to talk with God together in moments of triumph. The parent can calm the leaping, excited girl and say something like this: "Ginny, it's super that you made the team. I'm so glad. Let's say a prayer of thanks together." Then, holding Ginny's hand:

Thank you, God, for Ginny and for helping her make the team. Let her have a good year and help her win a few.

Again, this little prayer or one like it can be powerful in developing the relationship between parent, child, and God. If parents only understood the value of natural prayer in terms of the three-way interaction, they would use it more. It gives the parent an excuse to tell the child how pleased she or he is (or how disappointed), which is often hard for parents to do. It gives the child a chance to hear a parent share concern and pleasure over him or her alone. It gives both a sense of security in recognizing God as a member of the family.

Once the family gets accustomed to little moments of spontaneous prayer in the daily routine, it's a natural step to pray around a campfire, at the seashore, before a big event, and after a disappointment.

We will be talking much more about the use of spontaneous prayer in seasonal rituals. But for now, let me point out a few pitfalls. If parents are aware of these before beginning to experiment with prayer, some failures may be avoided:

1) *Don't put on a false face or voice while praying.* My son calls it a "church face." All of us tend to change our voice and our language when we pray. We get more solemn—and in some cases more pretentious and artificial. Try to work that out of your prayer life. The more naturally you pray, the more God becomes real to your family.

2) *Don't always assume a praying posture.* If prayer is to be natural, you should be able to pray while sitting in a lounge chair on the patio, while taking a walk, or while lying down.

Young children often define prayer as bended knees and folded hands because that's the only way they see their parents and other adults praying, and because the idea of spontaneous prayer is alien to their experience. As children often mistake the externals of prayer for prayer itself, it's valuable to model informal prayer for them.

3) *Don't wait until the children are around to pray naturally.* Children are very quick to recognize when something is done only for their sake. Breathe a prayer aloud during the day even when nobody else is around. Pray spontaneously with your spouse. This will make prayer more natural to you and

you will unintentionally pass on this comfort to your children.

4) Don't overdo it. I'd rather see parents not pray spontaneously at all than pray too much. Occasionally after a retreat or encounter weekend, parents will come back and turn the home into a mini-monastery, praying upon rising, upon washing, upon eating, upon going to school, and so on. The best word here is *gradual.* Learn to love prayer as a part of your family life by allowing it to develop on its own.

5) Don't force children or your spouse to pray openly. Spontaneous prayer has to be just that—spontaneous. It isn't spontaneous if we say a prayer and then stare at someone and wait for that person to come up with one. It isn't spontaneous if we say tersely, "I don't care what's on television, we're going to pray openly and lovingly *right now."* It isn't spontaneous if it's assigned. It isn't spontaneous if it's memorized. It defeats its purpose if the child—especially a teenage child—feels pressured to pray because the others are praying.

To avoid this, don't go around the table or from parent on down, but invite those who want to participate to do so. Don't rush anyone; make your children (and yourself) comfortable with silence.

It is well to remember that we are novices in this area of natural or spontaneous prayer. We grew up in a church of ritualized prayer, one in which we weren't expected or invited to participate beyond routine responses. Spontaneous prayer is, however, natural in many faiths. And people today are showing a great desire for it. The startling popularity of prayer groups and charismatic prayer attests to this.

Why not begin it in the family and allow it to grow in its own way? It can add a spiritual dimension to family life that has been missing for years, maybe even for generations.

CREATING
FAMILY RITUALS

Today's family has a great hunger for ritual. Paradoxically, we see parents denying any such hunger. Why? Probably because they are uncomfortable with the idea of celebrating God openly and naturally with their children. What we see in this kind of family is that the children eventually seek ritual and prayer outside of the family or parish circle.

Young Catholics are strongly attracted by charismatic groups and campus prayer ministries. Many teenagers and young adults regularly attend Scripture study groups in Protestant or unaffiliated parishes. Many of the young people explain their attraction to these groups in terms of the absence of real prayer and spirituality in their own faith, and particularly within their families.

How can the Catholic family replace the rituals and traditions lost since Vatican II with rituals meaningful to today's children? Most of today's families do not respond to rituals of an earlier age in our church: family rosary, novenas, and litanies. Most *do* respond to open prayer, song, and communal celebration. Our task as parents is to learn how to change, to adapt, to furnish new religious experiences in our homes so that our children will not have to seek them elsewhere.

One of my greatest pleasures in working with Christian parents comes from helping them instill a sense of ritual and celebration in a formerly sterile family religious climate. Although many approach first efforts with trepidation and sometimes apology, they soon discover that their children love it. To a child, once done is a tradition. Many a parent, after implementing a nameday celebration or family meditation for the first time, will hear one child say to another, "Oh, we *always* do that in our family."

Here are my "ten commandments for family ritual and celebration":

1) *Let the ritual serve the family, not the family the ritual.* We must not become enslaved to any rituals. Repeat that to yourself several times. Various rituals are suggested in this book. If you feel the words are alien to your family or that another order or combination of prayer would be more effective, by all means change them. God gave you your family, your common sense, and your faith. Combine them in the most nourishing way possible.

If a particular ritual does not emerge around your table as perfectly as it does in print, don't worry about it. There is nothing holy or enshrined about these rituals. They are merely words. The spirit your family puts into them—even when it seems untidy—is what makes the words come to life.

Our first family Passover/Holy Thursday meal was a disaster. I went all-out and used a linen tablecloth, candles, grape juice, the works. Our children were very young. I handed Jim, my husband, the stylized prayers and we began.

It bombed. The kids didn't understand the words. They spilled the grape juice and blew candle wax onto my beautiful cloth. I was dismayed and by the end of the meal felt a real failure. But everyone else thought the ritual was great. "Can we do it again next year, Mom?" they asked eagerly. That experience told me that I was trying to turn our informal family celebration into one worthy of a cathedral. Once I stopped trying to do that, our family rituals became more open, more relaxed, and more spiritual.

2) *Initiate at least one annual religious ritual in your family.* Tradition is what family is all about. Some marriages founder on whether gifts should be opened Christmas Eve, as it was always done in the wife's family, or on Christmas morning, as it was done in the husband's family. While there are daily traditions, such as how the family seats itself around the table or how it observes Saturday morning, usually when we speak of family traditions we mean traditions which surround special days or religious holidays.

Family therapists delve deeply into the sense of tradition in the families they are trying to help. The most solid, intimate families have many traditions: they celebrate each person's birthday in a special manner, they go to the mountains or seashore every Fourth of July, they invite the same people to baptisms and wedding showers, and so on.

I try to encourage each Christian family to develop at least one religious tradition that is uniquely its own. The possibilities are endless. Many are mentioned in Chapter Four.

3) *Rediscover and retain the ethnic religious traditions that are your legacy.* Once when I was speaking in Texas, Archbishop Patrick Flores heard me stress the value of religious tradition in the family. He said to me later, in his soft Spanish inflection, "As you were talking, I couldn't help but think about my people. They have such beautiful religious traditions but they feel they have to shed them in order to become truly American. Please encourage them to to keep these traditions alive in their families and in their homes."

Sadly, that's what has happened, not just among Hispanic peoples, but among the Italians, Basques, Irish, Polish, and

Germans who came to America. There seemed to be a race to shed the old world traditions that gave a sense of identity to the people, the parish, and the family.

I think of the Italians with their beautiful St. Joseph's Day custom of setting up food altars in their homes and inviting people to come, sample, and leave an offering for the poor; the Irish with their blessing of the fields and their wakes; the Polish with their Holy Saturday food baskets to be blessed for Easter; the Mexicans with the Posada at Christmas time. These and hundreds of ethnic customs too good to let disappear need to reappear in the family.

Check your roots and recreate a few of the more meaningful religious traditions in your home. Ask your elderly relatives about old customs. Visit the ethnic parishes in your area. If you have ties to several cultures, adopt what you like from each culture.

4) *Give your family rituals time, space, and planning.* Good family celebrations don't happen; they are planned. Look ahead on the calendar and schedule your lenten activities, your Pentecost brunch, or your summer meditation. Too many parents adopt the "we'll-get-around-to-it-sometime" mentality when considering family prayer and ritual.

Of course we will never "get around to it." We must *get to it now* if we are to initiate a sense of spirituality in the family before our children leave home and seek it elsewhere.

Sit down together as a family and decide what rituals you would like to try this year. Perhaps you will want only two: an Advent ritual and a family practice for Lent. Or perhaps you will be like our family, who celebrated the following occasions: Epiphany, Ash Wednesday, weekly lenten Stations of the Cross, family reconciliation services, Passover/Holy Thursday dinner, Pentecost, namedays, parents' wedding anniversary, Mother's Day, Father's Day, a Mary ritual in May, back-to-school, All Saints Day, Thanksgiving, daily Advent prayer, and various Christmas rituals.

Believe me, we never intended to have so many rituals in our family. But once the children got into ritual and celebration, they liked the intimate family bonding and looked forward to these times of sharing. Few of our rituals were long, maybe 20 minutes at the most. But they did require planning. Someone had to be in charge—my husband or I at first, but the children did nicely once they got old enough and familiar enough with the season.

Some families like to celebrate in the living room, others around the family table, still others outside if the weather cooperates. Find your family's special time and place. Scheduling time to gather today's family together all at once is a remarkable feat in families where the cheerleader has to leave before the paperboy gets home, or where family life becomes a series of notes on the refrigerator.

Often, the time directly after evening dinner or a Sunday afternoon is best for family celebrations, but you might prefer bedtime, before dinner, or Saturdays. Whatever you choose, do not try to work your celebration in before an important television program. It's defeating to condense a celebration meant to relax and bind the family into 12 minutes because Monday night football starts at 7:30 PM.

5) *Get a book or two on family prayer and ritual.* If you own this book, you already have one. If not, get one for yourself. Ask the director of religious education or the pastor in your parish to supply a variety of resources for families. You can't be expected to know prayers and rituals by heart, particularly if you don't have a history of them from your own childhood.

Remember that ideas beget ideas. Perhaps while reading some of the prayers in this book or in others you will be moved to write some for your own family. When I originally wrote this book, there were few resources for Catholic parents, especially ones which were easy, creative, comfortable, and appealing; but that has changed significantly. Today, thanks to God and publishers, there are many. Look in the Suggested Resources section in the back of this book for some of my favorites. I recommend that parents begin to accumulate a library of materials, maybe one book a year, for new ideas.

There are also some excellent newsletters and magazines for families who want to nurture an active spirituality in their homes. These have the advantage of being short, timely, and interactive. They are attractively presented, often with puzzles, games, and stories which can be utilized by time-starved parents who are unable to do the searching and researching for a specific celebration. The names of some of these periodicals will also be found in the Suggested Resources.

Videos are an excellent way of inching into family celebrations because families are already comfortable in sitting together in front of the television set. Most families have a video library of Disney movies and the like; but I notice that few parents are aware of the array of religious videos available for families and children. Look in back of this book for just a few of a wealth of value-oriented and religious-based videos.

6) *Share responsibility for celebration and ritual among all family members.* Ritual and celebration should not be Mom's job but everyone's privilege. If one parent, usually the mother, takes ownership of it, she finds herself in the position of having to beg, defend, and cajole other family members into participating.

Distribute responsibilities early. Even the youngest child can be made responsible for drawing a picture or choosing a song. Others can take charge of prayers, centerpieces, and readings. During Advent and Lent, let each member take turns being responsible for the daily or weekly ritual. Encourage children to originate ideas for new rituals and occasions.

7) *Strive for a blend of the traditional and the new, the memorized and the spontaneous, the formal and the informal.* Many Catholic families mistakenly believe there's nothing between

the family rosary and the charismatic prayer group. Yet there is a wide range of ways to express our faith. We can best teach our children and ourselves an enjoyment of and respect for the different religious practices and traditions by using a variety of such in the home.

Begin your celebrations with a comfortable old prayer like the Memorare, then continue with a spontaneous prayer to Mary. Sing an old hymn like "Holy God, We Praise Thy Name" along with "Here I Am, Lord." Read from an adult Bible and from a children's Bible. Pray a traditional litany, and then write one of your own.

In other words, keep the best of the traditional and pass it on to your children, but don't be bound by it, or by only what's contemporary. It's astonishing how many parents complain about their children's lack of familiarity with the old hymns and prayers without accepting their own responsibility to furnish opportunities for familiarity. The church didn't drop the rosary; families did. We can't blame the church for not teaching the Morning Offering or the importance of making visits to church if our children never hear us pray it or see us make a visit.

8) *Open your family celebrations to a wider family.* A religious sister once asked me if we ever invited sisters from the parish to be part of our family rituals. "No," I replied. "They probably get enough of that in their work." She corrected that impression at once. "We rarely get invited into families to be part of a celebration—only when we're there to furnish it. I would love to be invited as a guest to one of your Ash Wednesday rituals."

After that, we were sure to invite not only sisters but people whose families live far away, shut-ins, clergy, widows and widowers, single adults, and family friends. Now, when I work with families who are learning to celebrate, I encourage them to open the family circle to others. The very essence of celebration is expansion—beyond ourselves, beyond our own family, beyond our Christian horizons.

9) *Overcome awkwardness and embarrassment by celebrating first with those who are comfortable with it.* If you are one of those families who find it hard to pray or sing aloud together, to hold hands or to meditate together because you have never done it that way before, then ask a celebrating family if you can join them for an Advent or lenten ritual so you can see how it is done. Or ask your parish director of religious education or school principal for some demonstration celebrations or group rituals. Some parishes begin by having an Advent wreath ceremony the afternoon of the first Sunday in Advent for all the families in the parish. Families can then take the ceremony and the spirit of it home with them to replicate during Advent.

If you have teens it may be a bit harder to get a celebration started. Don't force them into anything. Invite them to help with the music. Usually they are quite good at that. Let the younger children lead you into the prayers and mood of celebration. Their sense of embarrassment isn't yet developed and their refreshing candor and participation can make the rest of the family comfortable.

If you have a spouse who doesn't want to be involved, ask him or her to join you but to play no active role until comfortable with it. Ask one of the children to do the readings, another to do the prayers, and so on. If your spouse refuses to have any part of a spiritual ritual at home, go ahead and have one anyway. Don't deny the rest of the family the experience simply because one parent is uptight. If the children ask why Dad or Mom isn't present, tell them you aren't really sure and suggest the child ask the absent parent.

(Unfortunately, the father is more often the absent parent. For too long, it seems, Mom has apologized for Dad in our church. In order to allow Dad to grow up in his faith, we must make him responsible for his own religious leadership in the family.)

10) *Help other families learn to celebrate God openly and lovingly.* Faith and celebration are meant to be shared. Once your family has tasted religious tradition and celebration in the home, you will want more. Avoid the temptation to nurture it for your own sake.

Once you feel you have established a comfortable degree of celebration in your family, offer to serve on the parish liturgy committee and suggest ideas to help other families learn to pray and ritualize together. Work at making Sunday liturgies more participatory. Invite a group of parents interested in home celebrations to form a small Christian community for ideas and support. In other words, take the blessings you have experienced from your family rituals and pass them on. That's the way the Good News gets spread.

4

CELEBRATING THROUGHOUT THE YEAR

The Times of Our Lives

For everything there is a season,
  and a time for everything under heaven.
Lord, let us make time for you:
  a time for a new year and a time for spring,
  a time for Lent and a time for Easter,
  a time for summer and for school to start,
  a time for Thanksgiving and a time for snow.
O Lord, let us take time to celebrate you
  in these times of our lives together.

The calendar is filled with events to celebrate. Holidays and holy days, the change of seasons and the recurrence of important dates—all these occasions and more offer opportunities for families to develop rituals of prayer and celebration. This chapter contains rituals for use throughout the year (separate chapters are devoted to the great seasons of the Church: Advent/Christmas and Lent/Easter).

Remember what I said in the last chapter: a ritual is only a suggested pattern for prayer. Your family's traditions will reflect your family's unique character. Always feel free to tailor my suggestions to fit the needs and preferences of your family. If you don't know or like a suggested song, substitute a family favorite. Add prayers of your own making, subtract drawings, modify these celebrations as the Spirit moves you—and trust that the Spirit does.

If you are beginning ritualizers, don't try to do everything that follows. Choose a few that your family will respond to most readily. Then, as your children ask for more, try a few more. Keep them short, reverent, and intimate. You will wonder why you waited so long to celebrate God together in your home.

New Year's Day

Opening song: "Sing a New Song," or an Alleluia setting

Prayer: Offer spontaneous prayers of thanks for the old year, and share family spiritual resolutions for the upcoming year.

Scripture: Genesis 1:1–2:4a, the Creation story.

Activity: Have each person draw a scene of their best family time or experience in the old year. Show and explain.

Closing song: "Let There Be Peace on Earth" or your choice

Martin Luther King Day

Opening Song: "He's Got the Whole World in his Hands"

Prayer: Prayer of St. Francis (see page 21)

Activity: Read aloud *Peace Comes to BW* by Jim Dinn and/or choose one of the activities from *Peace Begins at Home: Rituals and Resources for Peacemaking* from Pax Christi. Other good books include *Young Martin's Promise* by Walter Dean Myers (ages 4–7) and *I Have a Dream* by Margaret Davidson (ages 7–12).

Closing Song: "We Shall Overcome"

Presidents' Day

Opening song: "America the Beautiful"

Sharing: Ask each family member to tell a bit about the life of whatever president he or she chooses. (If parents take lesser-known choices, children can "be" Washington, Lincoln, Kennedy, etc.)

Activity: With butcher paper and felt-tip pens, together draw a large mural depicting God's blessings upon our country.

Closing song: "God Bless America"

St. Patrick's Day

This celebration can be planned around a meal with corned-beef and cabbage or Irish stew.

Opening song: Any favorite Irish song.

Story: Tell the story of St. Patrick's life from any book of saints. (This is a good time to get a saint's book if you don't have one.)

Activity: Pass out large paper shamrocks and draw symbols of the church, your family, and Ireland. Hang them when done.

Prayer: Use the following or make up one of your own:

The Breastplate of St. Patrick

Christ shield me this day:
Christ with me, Christ before me,
Christ behind me, Christ in me,
Christ beneath me, Christ above me,
Christ on my right, Christ on my left,
Christ when I lie down, Christ when I arise,
Christ in the heart of everyone who thinks of me,
Christ in the mouth of everyone who speaks of me,
Christ in every eye that sees me,
Christ in every ear that hears me.

Closing song: Medley of Irish tunes

Mother's Day/Father's Day

Opening song: "He's (She's) Got the Whole World in his (her) Hands"

Prayer: Homemade prayers written for Mom or Dad beforehand

Reading: For Mother's Day, read *Love You Forever,* by Robert Munsch; *The Way Mothers Are,* by Miriam Schlein; or *The Runaway Bunny,* by Margaret Wise Brown. For Father's Day, read *Papa Small,* by Lois Lenski; *A Day No Pigs Would Die,* by Robert Newton; or *A Father Like That,* by Charlotte Zolotow.

Prayer: The children can offer a spontaneous prayer
                   of thanksgiving for their parents,while Mom
                   and/or Dad tells why being a parent is such
                   a joy.

Activity: Recite a litany to Mary, our mother, or write
                   private notes of love to honored parent.
                   Then present the family's gifts.

Closing song: Mom or Dad's choice

End of School, Beginning of Summer

Opening song: "Morning Has Broken"

Litany: Each person is responsible for preparing
                   beforehand ten thank-you's for the school
                   year and ten prayers for the summer vaca-
                   tion; the family responds to each with,
                   "Lord, hear our prayer."

Sharing: Share individual and family resolutions,
                   beginning each with, "This summer I want
                   to...."

Activity: Divide a paper into four parts and have
                   each person draw two blessings (good
                   things) they received or that happened in
                   the past school year and two blessings they
                   hope to have in summer.

Closing song: "Amazing Grace"

Ascension Thursday

This celebration works well outside, if weather permits. It's
fine for the mountains, seashore, campsite, or backyard.

Opening song: "On Eagle's Wings"

Reading:	Acts 1:6–9, the story of Jesus going into heaven
Meditation:	Close the Bible and your eyes and meditate for a few minutes (see chapter on meditation).
Activity:	Have everyone lie on backs and share cloud shapes: "Does anyone see Jesus?"
Discussion:	Have each family member give their response to this question: If Jesus came back today, what would he be? (Example: "I think he'd come back as a school bus driver, because....")
Closing prayer:	Apostles' Creed (see page 14)
Closing song:	A setting of the Alleluia

Pentecost

Opening song:	"Come, Holy Ghost"
Activity:	Decorate Pentecost candles—each with one symbol of Pentecost: dove, tongues of fire, light, words, wind, rooftop, etc. And while you work sing together "Blowing in the Wind" or "We Are One in the Spirit."
At dinner:	Light all your candles and sing "This Little Light of Mine"
Prayer:	Come, Holy Spirit (see page 12)
Closing song:	"On the Wings of a Dove"

Mary Ritual for May

Opening song:	"On This Day, Oh Beautiful Mother"

Activity: Together, build a shrine to Mary for the
                     month of May. (Each member can take a
                     turn putting fresh flowers or little pebbles
                     around the shrine daily.) Then dedicate
                     your shrine with this prayer (or substitute
                     the traditional litany, novena to Mary, a fam-
                     ily rosary, or spontaneous prayers):

A Family Prayer to Mary

Come into our home, O most loving Mother Mary,
 and make yourself a part of our family.
Hear us when we are lonely.
Comfort us when we are sad.
Heal us when we are torn.
Celebrate with us, enjoy with us.
Share with us those moments of intimacy
    that transform a family
    from the mundane to the unique.
Honored Mother, invite your son Jesus
    into our hearts and our midst.
Let us reflect the light of his love
    in all that we do here at home,
    and let the rays of his love
    extend from our family to his family everywhere. Amen.

Story: Tell the story of Mary (use your Bible, if
                  you'd like, particularly Luke) and recount
                  some of the rituals parents remember from
                  their childhood, like May crowning.

Closing prayer: The Memorare (see page 19)

Closing song: "Hail Mary: Gentle Woman"

Fourth of July

Opening song: "This Land Is Your Land"

Activity: Present the flag. Take turns telling what the Fourth of July signifies. Say the Pledge of Allegiance together.

Prayer: Offer spontaneous prayers for the needs of our nation today.

Closing: A medley of songs such as "America the Beautiful," "God Bless America," "Battle Hymn of the Republic," "Star Spangled Banner," and "America"

Back to School

Opening song: "Peace Prayer"

Activity: Each child shares hopes and fears for the new year and the family responds with a Hail Mary for each child's year.

Drawing: A picture of what each person will be doing the following day. Parents should draw too!

Closing song: "Whatsoever You Do"

See the section "Prayers for School Days" on page 110 for additional suggestions.

All Saints

Opening song: Sing "When the Saints Come Marching In" while family members collect all the statues or pictures of saints in your household and put them in the center of the family circle.

Reading: Matthew 5:1–12, the Beatitudes

Response: Take turns creating "new beatitudes for today's saints." For example: "Blessed are they who pick up litter, for they shall keep our land clean."

Activity: Draw a favorite saint to exhibit and explain; or read from a children's saint book; or make a family saint poster or banner with each patron saint depicted. (If you do not celebrate namedays, this is a good day to tell the story of each namesake saint.)

Closing song: "Blest Are They"

All Souls

A visit to the church to pray for the souls of deceased relatives and friends is a good family ritual for this day. Before going, make a list of deceased loved ones and go over them with your family. Explain that God wants all of us with him in heaven and that we want to ask God to bring our dead relatives and friends ever closer to him.

If weather permits and your family likes adventure, you might want to borrow a custom from our Mexican and Filipino families by taking a picnic to the cemetery and having a joyous time with the spirits of our ancestors. This tradition helps children experience the reality that the world did not begin when they were born but that they come from a long line of chosen people.

Reading: Trina Paulus's *Hope for the Flowers,* an endearing book on life, death and resurrection. Other good stories on death include Pearl Buck's children's story, *The Beech Tree,* and Joan Lowery Nixon's *The Butterfly Tree.*

Closing song: "I Am the Bread of Life" or "Peace Is Flowing Like a River"

Thanksgiving

Gather before or after your big dinner but give yourself enough time to say more than just grace before the food gets cold.

Opening song: "Amazing Grace" or "We Remember"

Thanksgiving: Offer a family litany of thanksgiving, with each person responsible for ten items (people, things, events, and the like) for which they are grateful.

Prayer: Invite each person at the table to offer a prayer for others with whom we can share more of God's gifts and life.

Blessing: Parents ask God's blessing on the family so that each person remembers to thank God continually for his goodness.

Reading: Matthew 7:7–12, on God's care

Closing song: "This Land Is Your Land" or "America, the Beautiful"

Wedding Anniversary

Opening song: "Sunrise, Sunset" or the parents' favorite love song

Activity: Share wedding photos, while parents tell about the wedding: how they chose the date, who was there, who celebrated the wedding Mass, etc. (children love to hear these details).

Reading: John 2:1–11, the marriage feast at Cana

Renewal of vows: Parents join hands and recite vows (see page 121).

Response: Children offer prayers and/or gifts.

Closing: Family joins hands and sings "The Wedding Song" or any other favorite song appropriate to an anniversary.

Nameday

This is the celebration of the feastday of the child's or parent's patron saint. We celebrate much as we do a birthday, with a cake at the end of the meal and a story about the saint's life.

Through the years we have purchased a book and a statue for each of our children's saints: Teresa, Patrick, and Daniel. (These make a fine first Eucharist or Reconciliation gift.) We ask the children themselves to draw placemats for the meal with symbols and scenes from their saints' lives to give each familiarity with his or her saint. We ask them to write personal prayers to their patron saints to read right before the cake is cut. This is a good occasion to invite the godparents, too, if they are close by.

Family Reconciliation or Penance Ritual

Opening song: "Prayer of St. Francis" or "Bridge Over Troubled Waters"

Prayer: Come, Holy Spirit (see page 12)

Meditation: A parent invites all to quietly examine their consciences, or parents can offer the following questions. (A silent pause should follow each question):

What have I done to offend God?
What have I done to offend my family?
What have I done to offend others?
What have I failed to do as a Christian?
How can I let Christ's message shine through me?
What can I do to let God know I'm sorry?
What promises do I make to be a better Christian?

Prayer: Recite together the Act of Contrition (see page 13)

Reading: Luke 15:11–32, the prodigal son

Closing prayer: Prayer of St. Francis (see page 21)

Closing song: "Amazing Grace"

Parent's Blessing

A lovely family custom is a bedtime benediction. Make a little cross on your child's forehead when tucking the child in or saying goodnight. Then say this beautiful blessing from Scripture:

The Lord bless you and keep you!
The Lord let his face shine upon you,
    and be gracious to you!
The Lord look upon you kindly,
    and give you peace! (Numbers 6:24–26)

OBSERVING ADVENT, CHRISTMAS & EPIPHANY

A Christmas Promise

I have come to bring you peace:
  not the peace of the season, for it is too fleeting
  not the peace of the carol, for it is nostalgic
  not the peace of the greeting card, for it is too slick
  not the peace of the crib, for it is too wistful.
Rather, I have come to bring you peace:
  peace of the ordinary, the daily, the homely
  peace for the worker, the driver, the student
  peace in the office, the kitchen, the farm.
I have come to bring you peace:
  the peace of accepting yourself as I have fashioned you
  the peace of knowing yourself as I know you

the peace of loving yourself as I love you
the peace of being yourself as I am who am.
I have come to bring you peace:
  the peace that warms you at the completion of a task
  the peace that invades you at the close of the day
  the peace that sustains you at the beginning of the day
  the peace that comes when family members
  are reconciled.
Without peace
  my coming is unfulfilled
  my birth is forgettable
  Christmas is a contradiction.
I have come to bring you peace.

Planning Advent

The more I work with parents the more I discover a universal feeling of disappointment in the family observance of Christmas. "Every year we say that we're going to focus on the meaning of the Nativity," said a typical parent, "but we're so caught up in programs and gifts and parties that we never quite get around to Jesus."

The antidote to this disappointment is the insight that if Christmas is to mean anything in the Christian family, it must be joined with Advent and Epiphany. They are a trilogy, separate but linked.

At one time, few families observed Advent and even fewer the Epiphany. But today, most parishes place a great emphasis on celebrating Advent. This focus on Advent as an important time of waiting has carried over into many homes, as well.

In this chapter I offer three formats to help families observe Advent: a traditional Advent wreath ritual, a Jesse Tree ritual, and a modern format for an Advent celebration. I suggest you read all three and choose the parts of each which fit your fam-

ily. Then tailor yourself an Advent ritual that can become as traditional in your family as the Christmas tree.

Consider several factors before you launch into an Advent
celebration:

1) *Advance planning.* Plan far enough in advance so that
Christmas doesn't arrive in your home before Advent does. For
many of us, Advent comes before we are ready. More often
than not, the first Sunday of Advent is the Sunday after
Thanksgiving, a day given to closing a long weekend, to planning for Christmas cards and gifts, and to football.

If the family lets that first Sunday slip by, it all too often
shrugs its collective shoulders and figures it's too late to start an
Advent ritual. Try to start pairing Advent with Thanksgiving in
your seasonal mind. When you think Thanksgiving, think also
Advent—or the beginning of the Christmas season. We already
consider Thanksgiving weekend the beginning of the commercial Christmas season. Why not the beginning of the *sacred*
Christmas season?

2) *Family schedules.* Presume that there will be evenings that
your family will be unable to celebrate Advent. December is
filled with school and parish programs, parties, and other activities, so it's foolish to think that a family is going to be able to
gather together for a month of uninterrupted nightly rituals.
Rather, plan to hold an Advent observance on as many
evenings as possible in your family and be satisfied with that.
Remember my earlier reminder: the ritual is meant to serve the
family, not the family the ritual.

3) *Variety.* Strive to vary the evening rituals. We always took
turns planning Advent celebrations in our family so that the
routine didn't become meaningless. Even the youngest child
can offer a refreshing change of pace to the evening ritual,
because Advent—with its dominant theme of waiting and
expectation—is understandable to children.

4) *Balance.* Try to emphasize the idea in your home that

Advent is the foundation upon which Christmas is built. Stress the feeling of emptiness in people who have only tinsel and gifts for Christmas because they don't believe in God or who have no way of living out that belief. At the same time, don't overemphasize Advent so that the joy and wonder of Christmas gets lost. A practical and effective way of balancing both is by bringing the Nativity into routine Christmas traditions like decorating the tree. More on that later.

5) *Simplicity*. Remember that at this time of the year, which can be hectic and confusing in many families, we long for spaces of quiet and intimacy. Take advantage of this hunger in planning simple Advent rituals.

6) *Brevity*. This is a repeat of an earlier suggestion: keep the rituals short, even shorter than your usual prayer services. Children tend to be excessively stimulated during this month, so don't overdo it. An intimate, settling period of 15 minutes with the family gathered around the manger or Advent wreath could offer the salvation of sanity in the pre-Christmas family, while simultaneously focusing on the sacredness of this season.

Advent Wreath

The Advent wreath itself is simply a circle of greens holding four candles. Fresh greenery is preferable, but if you live in an area where greens are not readily available, use what you can. The base holding the greens can be made of just about any-thing—wood, styrofoam or coat hangers bent straight and then formed in a circle. If you have a handy youngster in your home, ask him or her to try fashioning a wreath base. Ask another child to place the greens on it, and another the candles.

Tradition dictates three purple candles and one pink (for the third week, called Gaudete Sunday). In our house, however, we used four white candles, one with a small purple bow around the base. My husband and I had received a Hummel infant as a wedding gift, which we would put inside the circle of the wreath. You may want to do the same, using a little crib set or statue of the infant Jesus that can be placed reverently inside by little hands. Or you can change the center decoration as the season moves on. On the first day of Advent, point out the symbolism of the wreath:

—The four candles represent the thousands of years that the Hebrew people waited for Christ's coming and, of course, the four weeks of Advent.

—The unlighted candles represent the dark ages before Christ's coming.

—The lighted candles represent Christ, the Light of the World. Each week we light one more candle to represent the idea that the coming of Christ is closer.

—The circular form of the wreath symbolizes that God has no beginning or end.

—The green of the boughs indicates hope, just as the green of spring indicates new life.

—The word *advent* means "coming" or "promise."

Traditional Advent Wreath Ceremony

On the first Sunday of Advent, the family gathers for the blessing of the wreath. Traditionally, the father is the presider (leader), but adapt this to suit your family:

Leader: Our help is in the name of the Lord.

All: Who made heaven and earth.

Leader: Let us pray. O God, all things are made holy by your word. Pour forth your blessing upon this wreath. Grant that we who use it may prepare our hearts for the coming of Christ and may receive abundant graces from you through Christ, our Lord.

All: Amen.

The leader sprinkles the wreath with holy water. The youngest child lights the first candle and the prayer for the first week is said:

Leader: Let us pray. O Lord, we ask you to stir up your power and come; that by your protection we may be saved from the dangers that threaten us because of our sins. Through Christ, our Lord, who lives and reigns for ever and ever.

All: Amen.

Leave one candle burning during the evening meal, at family prayers, or before bedtime.

Two candles are lighted on the second Sunday by the oldest child and allowed to burn as before. The prayer for the second week is:

Leader: Let us pray. O Lord, stir up our hearts that we may prepare for your only begotten Son, that through his coming we may be made worthy to serve you with pure souls. Through Christ, our Lord, who lives and reigns for ever and ever.

All: Amen.

Three candles are lighted on the third Sunday by the mother. The prayer for the third week is:

Leader: Let us pray. We humbly beg you, O Lord, to listen to our prayers and, by the grace of your coming, bring light into our darkened minds. Through Christ, our Lord, who lives and reigns for ever and ever.

All: Amen.

All four candles are lighted on the fourth Sunday by the father and allowed to burn as before. The prayer for the fourth week is:

Leader: Let us pray. Stir up your power and might, O Lord, and come. Rescue us through your great strength so that salvation, which has been hindered by our sins, may be hastened by the grace of your gentle mercy. Through Christ, our Lord, who lives and reigns for ever and ever.

All: Amen.

That is the traditional Advent wreath ritual. It is patterned after the Mass with the father taking the place of the priest as presider, and the family responding as if they were in the pews. Even the prayers come from the Latin Mass; they are the opening prayers. No songs, no spontaneous praying, no stories—just prayers in the formal language of the church.

This prayer service with the Advent wreath can be very effective if used during Advent as a sign of tradition. Parents can point out that this was the ritual that came down through the centuries. The words were translated into many different tongues, but all around the world Catholic families prayed the same prayers to the same God.

Jesse Tree

Although the Jesse tree is rich in Old Testament lore, it's fairly new to Catholic families as a ritual. Yet it is one of the most popular with today's families, and it is an excellent way of teaching Bible history to our children.

Simply put, the Jesse tree is Jesus' family tree. The term comes from the scriptural phrase "root of Jesse" (see Isaiah 11:1), from which Jesus ultimately sprang. So while awaiting the coming of Jesus during Advent, it makes a lot of sense to talk about the people who waited throughout history for him: Adam and Eve, Noah, Moses, Abraham, Isaac, Sarah, and the rest.

Families can use a Jesse tree along with or instead of the Advent wreath nightly until Christmas, hanging a symbol and telling the story of each Old Testament figure. It offers families a spiritual alternative to purely secular Christmas activities.

About two weeks before the first Sunday in Advent, start to make symbols for the Jesse tree. Use colored paper, felt markers, poster board, tempera paint, modeling clay, yarn, or other materials to make the symbols. Here is a partial list of biblical characters and symbols to choose from:

> Adam and Eve: tree, serpent, apple
>
> Noah: ark, dove, animals
>
> Abraham: sword, mountain, torch
>
> Isaac: bundle of twigs, ram
>
> Judith: sword
>
> Jacob: ladder, angels
>
> Joseph: bucket, well, multicolored robe
>
> Moses: basket, burning bush, lamb, staff, cloud
>
> Daniel: lion
>
> Jesse: root or bush
>
> David: slingshot, harp, six-pointed star
>
> Mary: lily, crown

You can find other figures by leafing through your Bible.

Gather a group of friends or families in your home (or at the parish) the afternoon of the first Sunday of Advent to hold a Jesse tree celebration. (If you can't get a group together, begin your Jesse tree celebration on this day with your family.) Before the event tell everyone in the group to:

> • make and bring several symbols to hang on the Jesse tree (these can be assigned ahead of time);
>
> • have family members ready to explain each symbol;
>
> • have another family member ready to read a short biblical account of its Old Testament figures;

• bring cookies or cupcakes decorated with the symbol.

One family might also volunteer to furnish a Jesse tree, either a large limb or a construction paper, wood, or felt tree large enough to hold the symbols. The Jesse tree celebration that follows is suitable for the family alone or for groups of families.

Jesse Tree Celebration

Opening song: "O Come, O Come Emmanuel"

Leader: After first explaining what an ordinary family tree is, explain that, for centuries, Jesus' family tree developed while people hoped and waited for him. Then give a brief explanation of the Jesse tree custom.

Reading: Isaiah 11:1,6–7: "A shoot shall sprout from the stump of Jesse."

Song: "Angels We Have Heard on High"

Symbols: Each head of family identifies the family by surname and symbol and introduces each member of the family to the group. One member reads the scriptural passage corresponding to its symbol, another explains the symbol, and another hangs it on the tree. If you are doing this within your family, have each member hang a symbol, then tell what it represents.

Closing song: "Joy to the World"

The celebration ends with decorated cookies and punch. (For a parish event, furnish plain paper and table space for families to make copies of other families' symbols for their own Jesse tree celebration. Encourage them to use it along with the Advent wreath on succeeding nights before Christmas.)

Modern Advent Ritual

The following ritual, while using the Advent wreath as a focus point, is extremely flexible. It can expand to include Jesse tree symbols and crib figures or be used as a simple ritual before the evening meal.

Before lighting the candle on the first day of Advent, have all extend hands over the wreath and say in unison:

Blessed are you, O Lord God, for you give us darkness, hope, light, and love.

Then pick and choose the elements from the following format that suit your family:

Opening song: "Prepare Ye the Way of the Lord" or "O Come, O Come, Emmanuel" or any Christmas carol

Reading: A Bible story from a book like Tomie dePaola's *Book of Bible Stories* or *Hark! A Christmas Sampler,* by Jane Yolen, or a Scripture reading such as the story of Elizabeth (Luke 1:5–24, 39-80), the Annunciation (Luke 1:26-38), or the birth of Jesus (Luke 2:1–21).

Activity: Draw a picture of some event leading up to the Nativity or of your family's pre-Christmas preparations. Share. Or write a promise to do something especially nice for a secret Advent friend in the family, or write a homemade family Advent litany (see Chapter Two on spontaneous prayer).

Prayer: A short meditation or spontaneous prayer of some type

Jesse symbol:	Prepare Jesse symbols beforehand, and place in a box. Have one child reach into the Jesse box, remove a symbol, and try to tell what it means. Suspend the symbol from a tree or doorway.
Crib figure:	Have one child dip into the crib box and take out a figure to build the Nativity scene gradually during Advent. Save the Infant for the last Advent ceremony.
Closing song:	"Soon and Very Soon," or a favorite family Christmas carol

Make this basic format even more flexible by rotating leaders and trying to outdo each other in creativity. You can turn out all the lights except the Advent candles and wonder aloud about how it must have been waiting all those years for the Savior or how it was in the manger that night. Once our daughter obtained a long sheet of freezer paper and we spent the whole evening drawing a Christmas mural together. It was a lot of fun and nobody wanted to quit.

We laugh when we recall one Advent when our youngest was very young indeed but wanted his turn to lead the ritual. The big night came. Under his direction we sang *Gloria*—just the one word—endlessly. Then he told a story of how the Three Kings came to visit Jesus in a dune buggy—and he was entirely serious! (In the toddler mind, what better way to get over the sand?) Then he had us take the animals out of the crib for a walk around the darkened house. We walked through the rooms dozens of times holding a cow or sheep and singing *Gloria.*

The last evening can be very special. On Christmas Eve, gather the family and any visiting relatives and friends around the wreath, say some prayers, sing some carols, and take the Infant from the box and put him in the crib. Allow the Advent candles to burn down.

Making the Most of Secular Customs

Here are some simple prayers and suggestions designed to turn your secular observances of Christmas into prayerful ones.

Tree-Decorating Celebration

All gather around the bare tree and pray:

Our Father, who gives us trees and all beautiful things, thank you for this tree. Help us to decorate it with excitement and joy in anticipation of your Son's coming. Lead us not onto each other's toes but help us realize how lucky we are to have one another, a tree, and you. Amen.

When the tree is decorated, turn on the lights and sit on the floor around it as you all extend your hands and bless the tree in these words:

Bless this tree, O Lord God, and let it fill us with the wonder and joy of Christmas, which is the gift of your Son Jesus to us. Amen.

Sing a few carols and then put away all the boxes and other litter.

Package-Wrapping Celebration

Gather around the table laden with tape, colorful bows, and presents. Pick someone to lead this prayer:

Holy Spirit, fill our hearts with love for the persons who will receive our gifts. Lord Jesus, guide our fingers to tie sturdy bows and our souls to anticipate your rebirth in us. Amen.

Sing carols as you wrap presents together.

Cookie-Baking Celebration

Gather in the kitchen around the table dusty with flour. As you roll, cut, decorate, and sample, invite everyone to offer spontaneous prayers of petition in the form of a Christmas litany:

Prayer: For safe Christmas traveling, we pray to the Lord...

Response: Lord, hear our prayer.

Prayer: For many more Christmases together, we
                     pray to the Lord...

Response: Lord, hear our prayer.

Christmas Mass for Children

The sacred part of Christmas is very hard to preserve on
Christmas Day. The kids are either too excited or too exhaust-
ed for any more ritual. I like the growing practice of having a
parish children's Christmas Eve Mass on the afternoon of the
day before Christmas, and then allowing the children to enjoy
Santa Claus, gifts, and relatives without trying to get them back
for Mass on Christmas Day.

If your parish doesn't have a special family or children's
Mass, perhaps you could suggest one. Some delightful customs
are arising at such Masses. Many include a reenactment of the
Nativity by children of the parish. Others have the children
bring up gifts which they have made to share with less fortunate children. Others have children invite their grandparents to
sit with them or, lacking grandparents, to substitute an older
friend in the parish or neighborhood.

The Stations of the Crib

I wrote this variation on the lenten practice of the Way of the
Cross for one of my columns a few years back. Use this on
Christmas Day, or on another evening following your Christmas
celebration.

First Station: Mary Says Yes

*We adore you, O Jesus, and we bless you, for by your holy
birth you have given light to the world.*

An angel appeared to Mary and said, "Don't be afraid, Mary,
for God has a surprise for you. You will become pregnant

and give birth to a son, and you will name him Jesus. He will be great and will be called the Son of the Most High God." And Mary said, "Okay, I am God's servant and I will do as He wishes."

Thank you, Mary, for saying yes, even though you must have been surprised and a little scared. Help us to say yes, too, when God calls us.

Second Station: A Trip to Bethlehem
We adore you, O Jesus, and we bless you, for by your holy birth you have given light to the world.
At that time Emperor Augustus sent out an order for all the citizens to register for the census, so Joseph and Mary went from their home in Nazareth to Bethlehem. What a difficult trip it must have been for this young couple, knowing they would be alone when Mary had her baby.

O Jesus, help us to trust in God's care when we face the unknown, as they did.

Third Station: No Room in the Inn
We adore you, O Jesus, and we bless you, for by your holy birth you have given light to our world.
While they were in Bethlehem, Mary gave birth to Jesus and laid him in a manger because there was no room for them in the inn. How sad Mary must have felt, knowing that this babe lying on straw in a place for animals was the Savior of the world.

Dear Jesus, help us to accept God's plan in our lives, even if we don't understand it.

Fourth Station: Angels Sing to the Shepherds
We adore you, O Jesus, and we bless you, for by your holy birth you have given light to our world.
There were some shepherds watching their sheep in the

fields that night and they suddenly heard some angels singing. They were very afraid but the angels said to them, "Don't be afraid. We have good news—a Savior has been born this night in Bethlehem. Glory to God in the highest and peace on earth to all of good will."

O Jesus, let us not be afraid of your angels and their words and let us always be of good will toward others.

Fifth Station: Shepherds Visit Jesus

We adore you, O Jesus, and we bless you, for by your holy birth you have given light to our world.

"Let's go to Bethlehem and see this new King," the shepherds said in great excitement. They found the baby Jesus lying in the manger. They told them what the angel had said and then they came back singing praises to God for all they had seen.

O Jesus, let us sing with joy your praises around the manger this season every year.

Sixth Station: The Wise Men Find Jesus

We adore you, O Jesus, and we bless you, for by your holy birth, you have given light to the world.

Three Wise Men saw a star in the East and followed it to the manger where they found the infant Jesus. They knelt down and worshiped him and gave him gifts.

How wonderful, O Jesus, to be recognized even as an infant and to fill us all with hope. May we always feel the gladness and joy that the Magi felt when they found you lying in the manger. And when we give each other gifts, may we always remember your birth. Amen and happy birthday!

Observing Epiphany

To complete Advent and Christmas, we need to observe Epiphany—and we have had little instruction on how to do this in our church and culture. For many families, Christmas ends with the Christmas Mass. Yet this is when the real celebration of Christmas should begin.

Try to leave your Christmas tree up until January 6th, the traditional observance of the Epiphany. (Liturgically, this feast is celebrated on the Sunday that falls between the second and the eighth of January.) If you do take down your tree before the sixth, move your Nativity set to be the center of attention. The simple act of moving the Wise Men a bit closer to the crib each day can be a start toward marking the Epiphany. Each evening have a prayer, a Bible reading, or a meditation around the crib. Sing some carols.

Make a visit with your family to various churches to view their Nativity scenes. With your children on vacation, daily Mass is worth considering. Have a *spiritual* gift-giving on Epiphany— handwritten prayers, small statues of saints or the Holy Family, banners, holy cards, or good deed offerings for one another.

Finally, have an Epiphany party in your home during which you exchange your spiritual gifts and take down the crib. Here is a simple ritual:

Epiphany Celebration

Opening song: "What Child Is This?" or "This Little Light of Mine"

Scripture: Matthew 2:1–12, the story of the Magi

Prayer: Individual prayers, each beginning with, "If I were visiting Jesus today, I would bring him the gift of...."

Gift exchange: Open and share homemade Epiphany gifts.

Activity: Have each person draw a big star and record a good wish for the family on each point. You can also take some chalk and write the

number of the new year plus the initials of
each of the Magi—Caspar, Balthasar, and
Melchior (eg., 19+C+B+M+97) inside on the
top of the main door to your home.

Closing song: "We Three Kings"

"LENTING" THE
WAY TO EASTER

A Family Lenten Prayer

Jesus,
 who went out into the desert to fast and pray,
 invade our hearts and our home during this Lent.
Be with us daily,
 increasing our self-discipline,
 hearing our prayers,
 and calling our attention
 to the good we fail to do.
Call us to be better people of God
 by praying and sacrificing for forty days
 in you and with you, forever and ever. Amen.

Recently, I visited some friends and, before I had even removed my coat, one of the small children proudly led me to their family lenten calendar. Fashioned like a large Advent calendar with little doors taped shut, it was displayed on a prominent wall in the kitchen.

"Every night we get to open a door," little Tony told me.

"And what do you do then?" I asked.

"Oh, we Lent," he replied.

I've thought of his answer many times since. I've never heard *Lent* used as a verb, but it's a perfect use for it because it is an action word. How many families actually "Lent" today? Oh, many of us talk about it, and most of us wish we did when it gets near Good Friday or Easter, but I'm afraid many children are growing up without any real experience of Lent.

When we were children we didn't necessarily like Lent, but we observed it. And I think it was good for us. It was a time for spiritual renewal of self, family, and parish. It brought us together in prayer and in ritual. Even families who prayed little the rest of the year took time out for prayer and sacrifice in Lent.

How does a family go about "Lenting" again? In this chapter, I suggest rituals that can be used in the family during Lent, some of them old, some new. You'll notice that I spend more time bringing the spirit of Lent into the home than bringing the family into the church. That is not to minimize church observances but to help you supplement them at home.

Ash Wednesday

Let's begin with Ash Wednesday. This ritual was a favorite in our family while the children were growing up. We would begin by making some kind of lenten shrine or centerpiece that would then stay in a prominent area of the dining room.

The motif varied from year to year. One year, my daughter took a large, round tray and divided it into pie-shaped sections. She filled one section with cinnamon sugar to symbolize the desert into which Jesus went out to pray (and I regret to say that the sugar steadily disappeared during the six weeks before Easter, possibly because we gave up desserts during Lent). In one section she put a small crown of thorns made of rose branches. In the others she put a cross, a little lamb, a towel bearing an image of Jesus' face, and a little mound of ashes. It was a convenient centerpiece because we could move the tray easily from buffet to table when we held our weekly lenten rituals.

Other years we had shoebox *tableaux* of the type that children make at school. One that my son made sat horizontally on the table and had the Stations of the Cross drawn around the inside (little hands can do that—adult hands can't) with the empty tomb made of clay on the base of the box. It was not only effective, it was also portable.

We don't use the word "shrine" much anymore, but that's essentially what these centerpieces were. The shrines of our childhood had two disadvantages for the celebrating family of today: first, they were personal (most of us had one in the corner of our room or in the garden, and it was considered *our* shrine, not the family's). Second, they weren't portable, so people had to go to the shrine.

Sometimes, of course, the whole family created a shrine and had some kind of lenten or Mary ritual around it. That's the prototype of the centerpiece I'm suggesting. We say "centerpiece" over "shrine" simply because it best describes it in today's language. We talk about centerpieces for our parties and other celebrations, so why not for a religious ritual?

Fashioning the centerpiece is a prayer in itself for the child and/or family. It's great fun for children to sit with parents and create something that is actually going to be used in a celebration. Don't just instruct your child to make a centerpiece; be ready to help plan it and create it if you are invited.

Begin to plan for Ash Wednesday a week or so in advance, asking the children (and ourselves) to clear that evening for our opening-of-Lent ritual. Then talk about the centerpiece, ask for volunteers to create one, and offer to help. If more than one child volunteers, suggest that they unite efforts or ask each to create something. If you end up with more than one, put them in different rooms of your house, then alternate using them for the main centerpiece.

Here is a basic order of events in that you can use in planning an annual Ash Wednesday celebration:

1) *Opening song.* After dinner cleanup on Ash Wednesday, gather around the lenten centerpiece at the dining room table and open with "The Lord of the Dance" or some other favorite lenten hymn.

2) *Family discussion.* Talk about Lent, for example, what it means and how it came to be observed. Here are some of the highlights you can cover:

• The word "Lent" comes from the Latin word *lecten*, meaning "spring." Its use goes back to the early church when the Christians-to-be were preparing to be baptized on Easter. They were called catechumens and, during the forty days prior to Easter, they repented, studied, and sacrificed.

• When infant baptism became common, Lent became a time of repentance and renewal for *all* Christians. It taps into the rich symbolism of the Old Testament, and recalls the time that the Hebrew people were waiting for their Savior to come. The Jewish feast of the Passover forms the basis for our eucharistic celebrations.

• The forty days of Lent, of course, come from Jesus' going out into the desert for forty days before he began his public ministry.

• Throughout the years, many customs have sprung up during Lent. Spring housecleaning is one. Remember that the Jews had to eat unleavened bread during the Passover. This meant they cleaned out their homes of all old yeast and prepared themselves for the new Spring season. This gradually became a Christian lenten practice.

• In some countries children plant grass seed in a box on

Ash Wednesday and put it in a dark place so that it will grow up white. Then they all take their boxes to church on Easter, and place them on the altar so that the whole altar is white.

• The custom of ashes comes from the old form of penance where the person publicly wore sackcloth (a cheap, uncomfortable shirt) and rubbed ashes all over to show repentance for some sin.

3) *Family resolutions.* Give concrete expression to your lenten resolutions by making a "lenten chain." Cut out strips of white paper about one by six inches in size, and give two to each family member. Discuss what you would like to do *as a family* to renew yourselves (see list of suggestions below). Then have each family member write down one of the suggestions; staple these into a lenten chain. Next, have each person write out a *personal* pledge of renewal and add these to the chain, which can then be draped around the lenten centerpiece.

Each week, repeat this process, writing down new family deeds and personal deeds, then adding the links to the chain. By Good Friday, when you staple the ends of the chain together, you'll have many links in your lenten chain. (Instead of the chain, some families make a large cross and tape pledges to it. Others fashion a lenten calendar like Tony's family did.)

Here is a sampling of the kind of pledges for family and personal renewal that might appear on your lenten chain:

• Give up sodas, beer, coffee, or tea one day a week.
• Walk to work or school or shopping one day a week.
• Make a daily visit to church.
• Go to Mass as a family once during the week.
• Read the Bible together 15 minutes daily.
• Babysit for a mother who never gets away from home.
• Eat one very simple meal weekly and send the money you save to the poor.
• Go to private confession during Lent or attend a parish reconciliation service.

- Say the rosary together once a week.
- Give up TV one day each week.
- Shovel the walks or mow the lawn for someone who finds it difficult.
- Listen to someone who bores you.
- Write a letter to someone who is lonely.
- Have a sugarless Tuesday as well as a meatless Friday.
- Make a family Easter banner together.
- Eliminate something that you enjoy: desserts, alcohol, snacks, or salt.
- Write a letter to a teacher or pastor thanking him or her for just being.
- Make a visit a week to the nursing home nearest you.
- Volunteer to collect money in your neighborhood for birth defects or some similar cause.
- Read one spiritual book privately during Lent.
- Hold a weekly Way of the Cross at home or together attend one held in the parish.
- Adults can fast for one complete day; children and teens can go without snacks for a day.
- Teach your children some prayers they haven't yet learned.
- Set aside one evening weekly just for Lent.
- Meditate 15 minutes a day.
- Do someone else's chores one day a week.

4) *Scripture.* Read the first two chapters of Exodus, which is the beginning of the story of Moses. During the following weeks of Lent, read two of the subsequent chapters in Exodus per week, continuing the story of Moses, Pharaoh, the slavery of the Jews in Egypt, and the plagues. This all leads up to the story of the Passover (Exodus 12–13:22), which can be read on Holy Thursday night. Use your family Bible or any good children's Bible, which tells the story dramatically and offers good pictures.

5) *Ashes.* My husband chars a bit of last year's palm from Palm Sunday and places a cross on each of our foreheads with the words, "Remember, you are dust and to dust you will return."

6) *Silent ending.* End your Ash Wednesday ritual silently, without a song. If you can, keep the TV off for the rest of the night, and take part in quiet activities. This gives the evening a somber but appropriate tone with which to start Lent. Give a pretzel to each person at the end of this ritual. Pretzels were created by a monk in the Middle Ages to feed the poor during Lent. The pretzel shape imitates arms crossed in prayer. (The Latin word *brachium,* from which pretzel is derived, means "arm.")

"Lenting" Together

At the beginning of this chapter, I told the story of Tony who said, "Oh, we Lent."

Later that evening, Tony's mother explained how their lenten calendar works. On Ash Wednesday, the family sits together and chooses an action for each day of Lent. Some actions are prayers, some sacrifices, some works to benefit others. They write down these actions—forty in all—on a letter-sized piece of cardboard. They then take a piece of paper of the same size, and fashion a handmade clone of an Advent calendar. (If you don't want to try making a calendar, write your forty actions on 3 x 5 index cards. Put the cards in a box, and draw one out on each day of Lent.)

"Actually the idea for the calendar is partially yours," Tony's mother said. "Do you remember your column listing family sug gestions for Lent? Well, we just took your list, adapted it to our family, and put it into a calendar form. Each evening at bedtime we talk about how we fulfilled our lenten pledge that day and open the little door for the next day. It keeps us moving on Lent, and the children especially love it."

I hope your family will begin "to Lent," too. Having some

weekly religious ritual at home is important to keep up the momentum. The easiest is the Way of the Cross which is printed below. Before or after you pray it as a family, check up on how you are doing in renewing and repenting. It's a long time between Ash Wednesday and Holy Thursday, and a lot of good intentions can fade if you don't gather and renew weekly.

There are several ways you can ritualize the Way of the Cross. Much depends on the age of your children. When our children were very small, we "drew" the stations on scratch paper while one parent read them. Then each person held up his or her picture at the end of each station. This is called "activity learning" and it is an effective way of teaching the Way of the Cross.

With older children, I suggest you invest in a series of booklets. If you live near a religious goods store, they will have a variety available. Or, you can ask your parish coordinator of religious education to order some for you and other families (I have a few suggestions for some in the resource section at the back of the book.) Or, you can simply use this Way of the Cross:

Family Way of the Cross
Let one family member lead this ritual. (Older children might take turns.) Then all join in with the response (you may want to make copies of the response for each person to read from).

Leader: Jesus, we come together to relive your sacrifice and suffering for us. Send your Holy Spirit into our hearts and into our midst.

All: We love you, Jesus, our Savior. We are truly sorry for having offended you. Never permit us to offend you again. Grant that we may love you always and then do with us as you wish.

Leader: ***The First Station: Jesus is condemned to death.*** Jesus is brought before Pilate to be judged, but Pilate is a weak and cowardly judge. Even though he knows Jesus is innocent, he is afraid of the powerful men who want him dead. So he washes his hands of guilt and condemns Jesus to death. *(Pause for reflection.)*

Jesus, never let us be afraid to do the good and right thing even if it means we will lose friends or suffer in some way.

All: Response...

Leader: **The Second Station: Jesus accepts his cross.** The heavy cross is thrust upon Jesus and he feels the rough heavy wood against his shoulders. He must carry the means of his own death to the hill, but does so freely to save us. *(Pause for reflection.)*

Jesus, never let us hesitate to take up our own cross, be it a disappointment, illness, or loss. You have shown us how to accept the cross with love.

All: Response...

Leader: **The Third Station: Jesus falls the first time.** How embarrassing it must have been to fall under the weight of the cross! Everyone was watching the man so many were honoring with palms just a few days before. It must have hurt to fall, too. *(Pause for reflection.)*

Jesus, let us feel your hurt and humiliation. Let us know that we often hurt and humiliate others deliberately and that isn't what you want us to do.

All: Response...

Leader: **The Fourth Station: Jesus meets his mother.** How awful it must have been for Jesus and for Mary, too. He knew she was suffering for him, this mother who wiped away the little hurts of

childhood with a kiss and a care. Along with the
big hurts of the cross, he had to worry about her
pain on seeing him suffer. *(Pause for reflection.)*

Jesus and Mary, you showed us how to love in
the midst of pain and degradation. Let us always
stand up to love even if it's the unpopular thing
to do.

All: Response...

Leader: **The Fifth Station: Simon helps Jesus carry
the cross.** Simon was grabbed out of the crowd
to help Jesus carry the cross, but Simon didn't
want to do it. He didn't know he was helping the
Son of God. *(Pause for reflection.)*

Jesus, let us see you in everyone we meet.
When we are tempted to pass them by even
though we know they are hungry or disadvantaged, nudge us as the soldiers did Simon and
give us the privilege of carrying your cross.

All: Response...

Leader: **The Sixth Station: Veronica wipes the face of
Jesus.** A woman—a mere woman in a time when
women were considered nothing—gathered up
the courage to run out and wipe Jesus' face. In
exchange for her love, tradition says Jesus gave
us his image on the towel. *(Pause for reflection.)*

Jesus, imprint yourself on us. Help us to be
courageous when we see others suffering, just as
Veronica was courageous in wiping your face.
She could have been killed; instead she was
blessed.

All: Response...

Leader: **The Seventh Station: Jesus falls the second** *time.* The cross is getting heavier and heavier. Jesus' strength is ebbing away, yet there is a long way to go. He falls and the soldiers prod him up again to continue his journey. *(Pause for reflection.)*

Jesus, it's hard to think about your pain and the weight of the cross. We say that if we had been there we would have helped you. But what if you were walking down our street right now and all our friends were taunting you? Would we help you, or would we join in with the crowd?

All: Response…

Leader: **The Eighth Station: Jesus comforts the women who cry for him.** The women who listened to Jesus in the streets and on the hilltops a few weeks ago now cry when they see his suffering. Always thinking about others, Jesus stops to comfort them. *(Pause for reflection.)*

Jesus, comforter of all, help us to do more than cry for others. When we see you cruelly treated in others today, give us the courage to stop the cruelty. Teach us to comfort those who are unloved in our world.

All: Response…

Leader: **The Ninth Station: Jesus falls the third time.** Jesus' strength is gone, and he knows it. He wonders if he can make it to the top of the hill. The soldiers poke and prod him with cruel taunts. *(Pause for reflection.)*

You must have wished to die there on the ground, dear Jesus. How cruel of the soldiers to taunt you. Help us to remember your perseverance. Help us to get up again when we have fallen from your love.

All: Response…

Leader: **The Tenth Station: Jesus is stripped of his clothing.** As if he weren't humiliated enough, Jesus was forced to disrobe in front of everyone. Even his clothes were taken away from him. Still, he showed us how to die with dignity. *(Pause for reflection.)*

You died with nothing, Jesus—with no money, no friends to save you, no honor, no clothes. Were you telling us something? That these things aren't really very important but that the love of God is?

All: Response…

Leader: **The Eleventh Station: Jesus is nailed to the cross.** How terrible the pain must have been. We hope that Jesus was numb so that he didn't feel every blow. Even so, he was still thinking of us and saying, "Father, forgive them, for they know not what they do." *(Pause for reflection.)*

Teach us to forgive as you forgave, Jesus. Sometimes we hoard little resentments and dislikes. Then we realize how you forgave and we take a tiny step toward love instead.

All: Response…

Leader: **The Twelfth Station: Jesus dies on the cross.** Jesus has died for us. For that he came into the world. In the words of the Mass, it is a death he "freely accepted." How can we ever thank him? *(Pause for reflection.)*

By your death, teach us to face death fearlessly, Jesus. Help us to comfort those who grieve. Help us to stop the senseless deaths caused by war and greed.

All: Response...

Leader: **The Thirteenth Station: Jesus is taken down from the cross.** Mary, who held the infant Jesus in Bethlehem, again held her bruised son in her arms in death. How terribly sad she must have been. *(Pause for reflection.)*

Hail Mary, mother of God, pray for us sinners now and always. Teach us to love as you loved Jesus and he loved you.

All: Response...

Leader: **The Fourteenth Station: Jesus is placed in the tomb.** Jesus' suffering stopped, and he lay in the tomb until that glorious first Easter morning. How joyful then his disciples, his mother. *(Pause for reflection.)*

Jesus, you have died, you have risen, you will come again.

All: Response...

Lent is an appropriate season for penance and confession. Instead of the Way of the Cross one week, have a family reconciliation ritual. This will be a meaningful experience for all, and will prepare your family for a parish penance service. (See the Family Reconciliation Ritual, page 52.)

Holy Thursday

The Holy Week services of the pre-Vatican II church hold strong memories for many older Catholics. These were somber weeks, filled with sacrifice, prayer, and reflection. Much time was spent in church, especially for the Holy Thursday Mass or service, and the traditional *Tre Ore* (Three Hours) on Good Friday with the Way of the Cross, sermons on the "seven last words of Christ," and kissing the feet of Jesus on crucifixes held out by the priests. Much of that has changed, but the spirit of Holy Week can be preserved in the family and parish if some effort is made.

Some parishes have a meaningful Holy Thursday liturgy followed by a parish supper. In many large parishes confusion rather than community marks the attempt. I much prefer a *family* Holy Thursday ritual.

In our home, we combined the Seder or Passover meal with the Last Supper observance to give our family a special sense of being doubly chosen: Old Testament *and* New Testament people. There are many Seder rituals available today. The one that follows is one that fit our family. Parts are borrowed from other rituals. Perhaps your director of religious education will give you a different ritual. Choose whatever is most comfortable for your family.

If, during Lent, your family has read the Exodus story of the Jews trying to escape the tyranny of Pharaoh and slavery, your family will better understand the meaning of Passover, the "passing over" of the Angel of Death who came to strike down the firstborn sons of the Egyptians but not of the Jews. After this terrible plague, Pharaoh let the Jews go with Moses to the Promised Land. If your family hasn't read the whole story of the plagues and Pharaoh, tell the story briefly and read from a good children's Bible the story of the Passover night itself.

Preparing for the Holy Thursday Passover meal should be a family affair, not Mom's job. Here are some of the responsibilities that can be delegated to various children.

1) *The Passover symbol.* God instructed Moses to have the Israelites mark with lamb's blood the top and the two side posts of their doorways so that the Angel of Death would recognize

them as Hebrew houses and "pass over" them. Have one of the children take a fat red felt marking pen, and on three pieces of paper draw a symbol that resembles a tick/tack/toe figure. (Or use another symbol, such as a lamb or unleavened bread or an Angel of Death.) Hang one on the outside of the front door, one in the room where you will eat your Passover meal, and one on the back door.

2) *Unleavened bread.* This can be baked or purchased. The traditional bread is the matzo, which is a flat, salted cracker that can be found in the kosher section of the supermarket, but any flat bread or cracker will do.

3) *Charoset.* This is a mixture of chopped apples, honey, and wine. It symbolizes the mortar the Jews used in building the pyramids for the Egyptians. An older child can easily be responsible for preparing this.

4) *Bitter herbs.* These symbolize the bitterness of slavery; horseradish is usually served.

5) *Parsley.* Symbolizes spring.

6) *Hardboiled egg and lamb bone.* These complete the Seder plate. The egg symbolizes new birth and the lamb bone sacrifice. Don't worry if it isn't a lamb bone. You can use a bone that you've saved from a chicken or roast. The egg should be sliced into as many slices as there are family members.

7) *Lamb.* We always served lamb on Passover night because it is so highly symbolic. You can cook a leg of lamb, or use shoulder chops or lamb stew.

8) *Table.* This night calls for your very best *unless* your children are very young. Arrange the settings as you do for important meals like Christmas or Thanksgiving dinners. Bring out the good china and silverware. Make a ceremony of preparing for the Passover, as our religious ancestors did. A centerpiece which captures something of the Passover and the Holy Thursday meal can be crafted by you or that creative junior-high child who's lounging in the doorway wanting to be asked

to be part of it all. A pretty tray with a wine glass, a little loaf of bread, and some representation of a lamb would be ideal.

9) *Lamb cake.* We were fortunate to have a friend who baked lamb cakes for us on Holy Thursday. We used this as our centerpiece. If you don't want to get a lamb mold, just bake a round cake and outline lamb-like features with icing. Tuck on some pink construction paper ears and you have a lamb—if you cock your head and squint a little.

10) *Guests.* Passover/Holy Thursday is a fine time to invite some of your close friends, godparents, and relatives, but you don't want a large crowd. That detracts too much from the intimacy of the observance. People who live alone may enjoy being part of this dinner. One child can be the official inviter, calling or sending invitations.

11) *Wine.* Because this is one of the few occasions we permit our children to drink a small glass of wine, we get a sweet wine. When they were younger, we used grape juice. There's not much difference in taste, but it adds to the ritual if real wine is used and they are permitted to taste a little.

12) *The Seder plate.* Directly before the meal, assemble the hardboiled egg, lamb bone, parsley, bitter herb, matzos, and charoset on a serving platter. If there are many at dinner, you can arrange individual Seder plates, but it's nice to share one large plate.

Here is the Seder ritual we used in our family:

Family Seder Celebration
Begin by lighting the candles.

Parent: Tonight we celebrate the Passover when God said to Moses in Egypt: "Tell my people: Every family must find a lamb. If a family is too small to eat a whole lamb, it should share a lamb with another family. The lamb must be young and without a mark on it. It may be either a goat or a sheep.

Child 1: "Slay the lamb and take some of its blood to put on the doorposts and lintel of every home of my people. That night they shall eat its roasted meat with bitter herbs and unleavened bread.

Child 2: "This is how you should should eat it: with your sandals on and your staff in hand, like those in flight. It is the Passover of the Lord. On that same night I will send the angel of death through Egypt, striking down the firstborn of the land, both man and beast, punishing the gods of Egypt.

Child 3: "But the lamb's blood on your houses will save you. I will pass over you; thus, when I strike the land of Egypt, nothing will hurt you. This day will be a great feast for you, which your children's children will celebrate."

The Seder plate is then passed and each item is explained. (See explanations earlier in this chapter.) Family proceeds with meal. When finished, remove all but bread and wine.

Parent: And so it was that before Passover, Jesus knew it was time for him to pass from earth to his Father in heaven. And so, during supper, Jesus, leaving us himself as a new sacrifice, took the bread, broke it and giving thanks said,

All: "This is my body which will be given for you. Take and eat."

Parent: Then he took the cup of wine and giving thanks said,

All: "This cup is the new covenant in my blood. Drink this in memory of me."

Parent: This bread and wine are but symbols of the holy

sacrifice, and we recall that each year our ancestors celebrated as we are celebrating tonight—
first the Passover and later the Last Supper on
Maundy Thursday. And each Sunday we rejoice
that we share in the Body and Blood of Christ at
Mass, which was begun tonight hundreds of years
ago.

*Each person takes some bread and wine. Candles
are extinguished. All sing "I Am the Bread of Life"
or another suitable hymn.*

Good Friday

Many families like to go to the parish service on Good Friday
afternoon or evening. Others prefer to stay home and observe
the afternoon in a family religious tradition.

For years we invited three other families and held a modified
"Living Way of the Cross." We used the format for the Way of
the Cross given earlier in this chapter, but we asked one family to bring large paper crosses to be pinned on the backs of
each child and participating adult, one family to furnish a
Veronica towel with an image on it, and another to furnish a
nonpiercing crown of thorns. Our children, as part of their Holy
Week preparation, drew the number of each station and placed
them in different rooms around the house—or outside if the
weather permitted.

The ritual itself was enriched by asking parents to take the
parts of Pilate, Simon, Veronica, and the others. At the Fourth
Station, each mother received her own little "Jesus." And after
one disastrous experience, we had the children genuflect
instead of fall at the appropriate stations. We passed over the
nailing to the cross which we felt was too traumatic. Instead we
held our arms out in a cross-like position while one parent read

the "Seven Last Words of Jesus" and explained them. Here they are if you would like to try this in your family:

Seven Last Words of Jesus
1) I thirst.
2) Father, forgive them, for they know not what they do.
3) Mother, behold thy son. Son, behold thy mother.
4) This day thou shalt be with me in heaven.
5) My God, my God, why have you abandoned me?
6) Father, into your hands I commend my spirit.
7) It is consummated.

At the "I thirst" words, we had an adult dip cotton balls in vinegar and touch the tongues of each participant. After being taken down from the cross, we sat on the floor in a tomb-like posture while someone read the following familiar prayer:

Prayer Before a Crucifix
Look down upon me, good and gentle Jesus, while before your face I humbly kneel and with burning soul pray and beseech you to fix deep in my heart lively sentiments of faith, hope, and charity, true contrition for my sins, and a firm purpose of amendment, while I contemplate, with great love and tender pity, your five most precious wounds, pondering over them within me and calling to mind the words which David, your prophet, said of you, my Jesus:

"They have pierced my hands and my feet;
   they have numbered all my bones." Amen.

Our children still recall our Good Friday Way of the Cross as meaningful religious experiences. Another way of observing Good Friday in the family is to read the Passion account together. If possible, borrow some of your parish missalettes and assign roles to each member of the family. Or, read the account directly from your Bible, using one of the following readings:

Matthew 27:11–54; Mark 15:1–39; Luke 23:1–49; or John 18:1–19:42. Open with a prayer, then read the Passion slowly and with meaning.

Note: At the end of each Holy Week, parish missalettes are sometimes thrown away. This is a good time to build up your family ritual library. Passover and Passion accounts (as well as Advent and Christmas prayers) can just as well be read from last year's missalettes as this year's. Ask your pastor or director of religious education if you can take some home with you at the end of the week to save for next year's Holy Week.

Easter

Easter is not a private family ritual but one that should be celebrated joyously at Mass with fellow parishioners and later, at dinner, with friends and relatives. If there are special customs that are part of your ethnic background, such as the Polish blessing of Easter foods on Holy Saturday, by all means continue those customs in your family.

An old custom familiar to many cultures is that of decorating Easter eggs. Many families like to do this together on Holy Saturday. Instead of just dyeing the eggs, try decorating some of them with religious symbols such as the tomb, cross, rising sun, Easter lily, and the like. (You can also decorate an Easter candle with similar symbols.) Choose the favorite egg of each child and make a centerpiece for your Easter dinner.

Some families like to make special bread for Easter breakfast. An old Italian custom is to bake a whole egg—shell and all—in the top crust. If this idea appeals to you, an easy way to do it is to buy frozen bread dough. Thaw and braid two loaves into one. Then prick an egg and place it in the center of the top crust just before baking. When the bread is slightly warm, glaze it with a powdered sugar icing. If you let the children help braid and glaze, they will more eagerly anticipate eating the bread on Easter morning.

7

FOSTERING
MEDITATION &
BIBLE STORIES

*In prayer it is better to have a heart without words, than
words without a heart.*

—John Bunyan

Two of the fastest growing interests in our church today are Bible
study and meditation, and until recently, most Catholics were unfa-
miliar with both. Not too many years ago the Bible was considered
a Protestant thing. Catholics heard the Gospels on Sunday and that
was enough for us. Meditation was mainly for monks, cloistered
nuns, and retreats.

Now we are discovering new excitement in both areas.
Catholics are flocking to Scripture study groups in their parish-

es or in other churches where people may be more knowl-
edgeable and more familiar with Scripture discussion tech-
niques.

Many of the other Christian denominations have a familiarity with the Bible that engenders a kind of open love for it
which is attractive to all, especially to young people. That is
why we are seeing so many young Catholics attracted to campus Bible groups. They are finding something there that they
haven't found in their own churches or homes, and it's more
than just a book. It's a lifestyle based on familiarity with the
Bible, something relatively new in Catholicism.

At the same time many youth and adults are also finding God
through meditation. The immense popularity of centering
prayer and guided imagery meditation attests to a need for
reflection and quieting. Certainly our hectic pace of life can be
blamed to some degree, but there's also a hunger for deeper
meaning—a search for God in daily life.

In this chapter I would like to pair the two—Bible and meditation—and give some suggestions for fostering them in your
family.

Bible Stories

If you have young children, invest in a good children's Bible
and/or a few Bible storybooks. You won't regret it. You'll find
yourself reaching for them during rituals and times of quieting.
Eventually your family will begin reaching for them too.

When our children were small, I invested in a set of little
Bible booklets, each containing a simple story and attractively
illustrated for children. Instead of keeping the little paperbacks
with our other Bibles and celebration books, I kept them in the
children's bookcases. They would reach for them occasionally
just as they reached for other books. Many a morning I found
one on the bed of a child who was supposed to be sleeping,
not reading, the night before. They have been used and reused

so much that when I wanted to give them away a couple of years ago, there was a collective protest from my grown children, who want me to save them for their children.

I could mention some popular children's Bibles, Bible storybooks, booklets, and Bible activity books here, but whenever I mention a few specific books, I risk omitting other very good children's and family Bibles. I really believe that certain Bibles are tailored to certain families and that your best move is to visit several church goods stores and secular bookstores and look over their selection before you invest. If you are buying a hardback Old and New Testament for children, check the binding and make sure it's sturdy. It will get a lot of bouncing around and opening flat on its face.

Once you get the Bible or Bible stories, what do you do with them? They are immensely valuable during the home rituals I suggest in earlier chapters. Help your family to become familiar with the Bible, first through the little Bible stories, later through readings, discussions, and meditation. Every time you are going to have a family ritual or special bedtime prayer, read from one of the Bible storybooks or a favorite passage from the Bible.

Familiarity is an important part of celebration. Just look at the difference in parish singing when a traditional hymn like "Holy God, We Praise Thy Name" is sung. People really sing those particular songs not because they are more musical or the words are more stirring, but because they are familiar to them. Our children will probably react similarly to the popular church songs of this generation.

During Lent, Advent, and other periods of the year, read a little of the Bible after each evening meal. Children love the Old Testament stories if they are on their level. In earlier chapters, I suggest using Bible stories as an integral part of Advent rituals, as preparation for the Passover/ Holy Thursday meal, and for numerous other church holidays.

One of the greatest helps for families is to have parents familiar with the Bible. If you count yourself among the thousands of Catholic parents who feel baffled in this area, why not seek out a good Scripture study group? Ask about one at your parish or get together a group of parents like yourself and find someone to lead you. Or you can look into some of the Scripture study video programs and books that are available. Lacking that, inquire about Scripture study groups in the other churches in your geographical area. You will find much ecumenical sharing in these classes.

You may have gathered by now how strongly I feel that every family should have a religious bookcase or shelf. This shelf would have on it all your Bibles, this book and any others like it, ritual paraphernalia, books about saints, old but useful missalettes, religious song sheets and hymnals, old and current religious textbooks (for reference), religious records, and any religious storybooks you may have. When a family member is leading a prayer session or ritual, he or she can go directly to this shelf and find the materials they need.

Meditation

Meditation came into the popular culture more than twenty years ago. It started out as a fad with the so-called "hippie" movement, but has now gained acceptance as a form of stress management and as an integral part of alternative medicine. Its use as a tool to help relieve everyday tension, as well as assist in the healing process during an illness or after an operation, is widely regarded in the medical industry today.

But the practice of meditation is not at all new to our church. The rosary is a prayer of meditation. The constant repetition of the same prayer while dwelling on a mystery serves much the same purpose as does a mantra in transcendental meditation—with the added gift, of course, of bringing oneself into God's presence.

While ours was not a meditating family, I found that we liked very much to settle our minds and bodies with quiet times together around a specific season or reason. For example, one of our favorite Advent rituals was to sit in front of the Nativity scene with only the lights of the tree glowing in the room. We would sing a soft carol, have a short reading about the Annunciation, and then hold a period of silence.

Your time for meditation doesn't have to be long: in fact, meditating with children is counterproductive if it is too long. Don't let your silence go much over four or five minutes until your family builds up to more time than that. Merely diminishing the stimulation of lights, noise, and rushing leads to a natural kind of meditation.

The car is a fine place for meditation. When we would travel, we read stories such as *The Velveteen Rabbit* when the children were little or a selection from Anne Frank's *Diary of a Young Girl* when they were older; then we just thought about it for a few miles before we talked about it. And just as the car is ideal for reciting the rosary, so is it effective for reading Scripture. Read the story of the prodigal son (Luke 15:11–32), for example, and let several miles go by while each person reflects silently on how he or she would react as son or father in the same situation. Then open things up for discussion. Many a pleasant mile can be passed in this way.

As I work with parents across the country, I find many families who frequently use meditation together. Often this is as a result of the parents' involvement in centering prayer, yoga, or some other form of meditation. Some families seem better able to pull it off than others. Those who have worked hard to get their families to meditate together tell me to caution families not to expect too much too soon, or to push meditation too strongly.

One father told me, "Actually, we didn't push the kids into it at all. My wife and I took a course in meditation from our diocesan adult education office. Every night after dinner we went into the bedroom and meditated together for 20 minutes. One night our teenager asked if he could join us. From that time on, it was just a matter of which child next. Now we all get involved, although not every night."

There are many ways to meditate. A good way to start is to gather the family together, then have everyone get comfortable and quiet. Turn the lights low (but leave enough light to read by). Then, read a short passage from Scripture, or from a book of meditations. After the reading, ask everyone to keep quiet for a few minutes and think about what they have just heard. Following this quiet time, you can have a brief discussion or simply end the meditation time with silence.

Some good books which offer meditations include *Moonbeam* and *Starbright*, two books for children by Maureen Garth, and *The Little Monk* by Harry Farra. For variety, try a children's meditation tape, like *The Dolphin Song* from Credence Cassettes. For those who can't obtain this tape, here are some suggestions from it for Scripture readings:

Luke 10:25–37	Luke 11:5–13
James 2:14–26	James 2:1–13
Matthew 5:21–26	Matthew 5:38–48
Matthew 25:31–46	Mark 10:35–45
John 14:15–31	John 13:31–35
John 15:1–17	1 Corinthians 13:1–13

To these I would add Psalm 23 ("The Lord is my shepherd") and Ecclesiastes 3:1–8 ("There is an appointed time for everything..."). You can also use any prayer that your family likes. I like to meditate with the Prayer of St. Francis ("Lord, make me an instrument of your peace..."; see page 21).

Here are some more suggestions for meditating:

1) Write individual prayers that are about the length of a Hail Mary. Read each aloud and reflect or meditate on each for two or three minutes before reading the next. (Parents, save these

prayers and present them to your children when they are parents themselves.)

2) Listen to a popular religious song together or sing a hymn from church and meditate on the words.

3) Read one of Tomie DePaola's books and meditate on the message for a few minutes.

4) Read a parable and have everyone draw a picture of it. Place the pictures on the floor or table so the group can see them and meditate on them.

5) Say the Apostles' Creed (see page 14) in segments, stopping after each phrase to meditate on its meaning.

6) Instead of bedtime prayers, sit together quietly and review your day or examine your consciences with the use of the questions from the Family Reconciliation Ritual (see page 52).

7) Recite a favorite proverb or motto, for example:

"Prayer does not change God, but it changes the one who prays" (Kierkegaard).

"To the millions who have to go without two meals a day, the only acceptable form in which God dare appear is food" (Mahatma Gandhi).

8) Take just one thought from Scripture and reflect on it, for example:

"I am the resurrection and the life. Those who believe in me, even though they should die, will live, and everyone who lives and believes in me will never die." (John 11:25–26)

9) Read one of the stories of a saint's life from a book of saints. Meditate on how easy or difficult it would be today to live the kind of life that person lived.

10) Holding hands, hum "Amazing Grace" for a minute or two; drop hands. Continue humming, breathing deeply and thinking of a scene from Jesus' life, such as his baptism by John.

11) Sit around a campfire or fireplace and tell about the moments in your life when God spoke to you forcefully. After each, stop, and meditate while studying the fire.

12) Go out into your backyard on a summer's night and lie down on the cool green grass. Search the stars with your eyes and talk quietly about the vastness of the universe and the wonder of the Creator who fashioned it. Drift off to solitude together.

These are just a few suggestions. None of them may fit your own family's style, but keep searching for what does appeal. Keep in mind that one of the expressed hopes of people for a more satisfying life today is for *less:* less confusion, less noise, less materialism, and less stimulation. We also want *more:* more time together, more time outside, more quiet time, and more time to get to know ourselves. Why not begin the process in your family?

EXPANDING PRAYER HORIZONS

We draw on many sources for our prayers. Some come ready-made from our rich heritage, others rise spontaneously from joy or anguish. Still others are formed and reformed by ritual until they are firmly rooted in a family's tradition. And that does not begin to exhaust the possibilities of family prayer.

This chapter offers a further sampling of prayers which reflect many moods and styles. Use it as a prayer book, if you like. Pray these prayers with and for your family as the need arises. Use them, too, to spark your own creativity and open your family's eyes to possibilities yet unexplored.

PRAYERS FOR ORDINARY DAYS

Prayer for an Ordinary Family

Thank you, God, for an ordinary family
  with ordinary problems and joys.

We don't seek the model marriage,
    the brightest children,
    or the best neighborhood.
We are content with the gifts you have sent us:
    normal children,
    a good marriage,
    and satisfying work.
For these, we thank you.
Let your light shine through our ordinariness.

Listening to God

Lord, teach me to listen for you
in the many ways in which you speak:
    in the phone call from the tiresome neighbor,
    in the drudgery of housework that will need to be redone
        tomorrow,
    in the inane and materialistic television commercials,
    in the flus and fevers of February,
    in elections, disasters, and deaths,
    in laughs, nonsense, and joy.
Let me believe, really believe, that you speak to me daily
in dozens of voices and forms. Then I won't have to wait
for that profound spiritual bolt of lightning to know you.
Then we can become good, everyday friends.

For Grandparents

For grandmothers and grandfathers,
    praise the Lord.
For the limitless love they share,
    for the concern they show,
    for the prayers they say,
    for the hope they pass on,
    praise the Lord.

For the lines and wrinkles,
  for the limps and liver spots
  for trifocals and bad knees,
  for gray hair and bald spots,
  praise the Lord.
For the birthdays they never forget,
  for the afghans they knit,
  for the memories they share,
  for the example they offer,
  praise the Lord.
For the babies they hold,
  for the stories they read,
  for the bragging they do,
  for the pictures they show,
  praise the Lord.
For the day, pray God, when we will be
  grandparents just like them,
  praise the Lord.

To Overcome Inertia

Help me to get moving, Lord.
I have boring work to do.
I did it last week.
I'll have to do it again next week.
Help me to find some pleasure in it,
  even if it's only to know that I've accomplished it.
Help me to understand
  that there are uninteresting jobs in everyone's life.
Teach me not to count how many times I've done this
  or how many times I must continue to do this,
  but rather to thank you for all the work I do
  that is not boring.
Help me to get moving, Lord.

For Help to Make the Team

Help him to make the team, dear God.

Oh, please, help him to make the team.

I know there are lots greater problems in the world—
    like wars and hunger—but he doesn't.

Right now, the only world for him is the team.

He's tried twice before and not made it.

He's getting bigger and beginning to doubt himself.

Oh why, dear God, must muscles and coordination
    determine the self-worth of a ten-year-old?

If he doesn't make the team, please,
    at least let him feel worthwhile.

Help him to understand he has many gifts and talents
    that the tough boys don't have.

And, if there's room for one more favor, God,
    would you give him some little way of saving face
    if he doesn't make it?

Maybe a conflicting activity or even a sore muscle?

Some way out so he can tell his friends and himself
    that he could have made the team if....

Thanks, God, for your patience with a mother
    who loves her children a little too much at times.

Prayer to Mother Seton

Congratulations on being a first:
    a first American saint who was first a wife and mother,
    then a Sister who went through all the pains
    of trying to be good in all your roles.

Most important to me, you are also the first saint-mother
    who had children who didn't turn out perfectly.

For that, I thank you.

We imperfect parents—
    or parents of imperfect children—
    need models of hope.

I know you worried about your sons.
So do we all.
You prayed one back into the fold
    but felt that you failed with another.
It's comforting to know that even a saint
    shared our feelings of failure and guilt.
Help us to do our best, as you did,
    and then to understand God's reasons
    for permitting us to fail occasionally.

For Something Lost

I can't find it, God. Please help me to think, to recall where I might have put it. I place my trust in you to help me find it. Lead me in that direction.

St. Anthony, who has helped us find so many things, I ask for your prayers too. And when I do find it, let me not forget to thank you.

Rain, Children, and God

It has been raining for eight days, God be praised.
It has ended a period of drought, God be praised.
It has brought new life to the trees and the grasses,
    God be praised.
Aye, it has been raining for eight days, God be praised.
It will soon cease, God be praised.
It is shortening the life of this graying mother
    and her penned-up offspring.
It will soon cease, God be praised!

Prayer Before Reading to a Small Child

Thank you for this bonus, Lord, this moment of intimacy and sharing between me and my child. Let me savor the quiet joy we give to one another.

Help me to make time to read together again tomorrow, because the day after tomorrow he will be reading
to himself and will be much too grown-up to pull my arm
around him and open a story that transports us together
to another time and place.

And for those families who have never read together, I
pray, Lord, that they try it just once. Amen.

A Child's Prayer to Mary

When I am scared or mad or blue,
Help me, Mary, to pray to you.
Because a mother always cares,
I know that you will hear my prayers.

A Mother's Prayer to Mary

It's morning, O Mother of mothers,
    and I face an impossible day.
Go to work, pick up the children, buy groceries, cook,
    clean the house, go to the meeting—
I don't see how I can get through this day
    without your help.
Mary, keep everyone well today.
Keep interruptions at a minimum.
Give me the courage to say no.
Most of all, Blessed Mother,
    nudge me to recognize the joys of this day,
    the glory of God,
    and the availability of you.

An Adult's Prayer to Mary

Mary, you said yes and we received.
We say maybe and wander in doubt.

Give us the strength of your faith,
   the confidence of your "yes,"
   and the courage to live the Good News
   as your son lived and preached it.

For Quieting the Mind and Body

I needed to stop and reflect, so I worked faster.
I needed to think, so I took a class.
I needed to pray, so I read a book.
I needed to retreat, so I called some friends.

   O God, Creator of silence and solitude, refuse me these
escapes from myself and from you. Let me heed your call
to retreat, to quiet my mind and body, to find peace in
your gifts of nature. Help me to be an example of peace
and harmony to my family.

Meditation Over a Sick Child

Two AM my vespers,
   cold kitchen my cathedral,
   rocking chair my kneeler,
   sick toddler my prayer.
Who needs a retreat master to explain
   that those hot little fingers seeking relief—
   roving constantly from my neck, to my shoulders,
   to my back and back again—
   are my soul seeking relief,
   roving constantly around God?
Who needs a canon and printed formula
   to teach me prayer
   when I hear such loving, trusting,
   entreating prayer from parched lips,
   "Mommy, Mommy, Mommy...."

Who needs a pulpit preaching patience
     when that,
     and love,
     is all I can offer?
Who needs lofty lessons on hope
     reflected off stained-glass windows on high holy days
     when hope is the divine balm of motherhood?
Press closer, little one, for comfort
     as I press closer to God
     for your comfort.
Merge into me,
     losing your pain in me.
Like God, I welcome it.
Whimper "why, why, why the pain?"
Dear God, why the pain all around us?
Why his tiny pain?
Why my mother's anguish over my helplessness?
Is it to show us we are helpless?
Ah, Mass is ended—he goes to sleep,
     wet brow, limp limbs.
From kitchen cathedral I carry him to warm crib.
I go in peace to my bed.
Thanks be to God for pain
     and relief of pain,
     which is love. Amen.

All the Other Kids Are Going
Here we go again, Lord—
     long face, swollen lip, wounded eyes.
Nobody understands her,
     this first child in all your world
     to hear "no."
Ah, the indignity of it all!

"My mother won't let me…"
"My dad's a square…
"It's too far…"
"Too late…"
"Too young…"
Sob.
Sob away, my child,
 and if it helps, hate me.
I know your anguish.
Yesterday I, too,
 railed at the unfairness of it all.
Too young, then too poor,
 then too married, then too old to go.
Go ahead and pout away, my love,
 for much of life is "no."
And one must rehearse, I know.

While Working in the Garden

"And he went out to the garden to pray."
I've always understood that, Jesus.
In my garden cathedral,
 I see your father's remarkable works:
 the balance of nature, the sprouting of seeds,
 the weeds striving for rightful space,
 the world in microcosm.
On my knees I work and reflect.
My garden is a prayer—
 not a perfect prayer,
 but then, not a perfect garden, either.
I love to work alone there in the quiet of a late afternoon.
It brings me closer to you, Jesus,
 and to your father
 who created gardens for our bodies and souls.
Let me always have a garden.

A Mother's Thank You

Thank you, God, for September
    for it ends endless August
    with its "there's-nothing-to-do's"
    and "I'm telling's"
    and "How-come-I-always-have-to's."
Thank you, God, for 98.6,
    for it ends endless fevers
    and their complications
    and sunken eyes
    and limpid little bodies.
Thank you, God, for Mondays,
    for they end the weekend
    with its basketball games
    and "everybody's going"
    and "I've got to be there by eight's."
Thank you, God, for bedtime,
    for it ends the day with its morning freshness
    and afternoon homecoming
    and evening sharing.
Thank you, God.

After Yelling

Mother Mary, help me not to yell so much. I couldn't help it. Maybe. After picking up all day, I couldn't stand the sight of those socks and shoes, dropped in a parade across the living room. I know I overreacted and said some things I shouldn't have said.

Give me the courage to apologize, but first let me feel forgiveness. I'm tired tonight and I'm feeling sorry for myself. Why do I take one's faults out on all of them? They're tiptoeing around out there feeling guilty. Don't let me enjoy that so much.

Sometimes I wish I could walk out the door and be responsible for myself alone: no more littered floors, no more bickering children, no more dirty pans.

No more cuddly children? No more shared laughs? No more of those who make my life worthwhile? I don't really mean it, Mary. But help me not to yell so much, please.

Everyday Marriage Prayer
Lord, let not our marriage become stale and meaningless, a convenient shelter for married strangers.

Let us, rather, seek and find ever new joy and wonder in one another, reliving the excitement of our early discovery of love together. Help us to make you the foundation of our marriage, the nuptial band that surrounds our love and keeps it sacred.

On a Beautiful Day
What a beautiful day it is, Jesus. Let me appreciate you in every nerve, every waft of refreshing breeze, every shout of playful noise from my children, every smile from my spouse. Thank you for this day and for your glory in it.

PRAYERS FOR SCHOOL DAYS

A Prayer Before the First Day of School

First parent: School starts tomorrow, Mary. We put this year in your hands.

Second parent: We pray that our family will emerge in June more learned, more prayerful and more compassionate to others.

Each child: That I will like my new teacher, that my new teacher will like me, and that I will learn all that I am supposed to in this grade,

All: Please pray to Jesus for us, Mary.

Parent: That all children everywhere will experience loving teachers and good classes,

All: Please pray to Jesus for us, Mary.

Each teen: That my school year will be filled with good classes, good friends, exciting school activities, and God's love,

All: Please pray to Jesus for us, Mary.

Parent: That we have a minimum of illness, unfinished homework, and missed buses,

All: Please pray to Jesus for us, Mary.

Parent: That our children will help new children to be less lonely and less frightened these first days of school,

All: Please pray to Jesus for us, Mary. Hail Mary, full of grace, hear our prayer for a school year that will please your Son, educate us, and help us to fulfill God's plan for us in his world. Amen.

Parent-Teacher-Student Litany

> *Leader:*   Dear God of all Creation, thank you for the marvelous gift of learning. We beg you to hear our prayers for our school life. Come into our midst, into our minds and into our hearts.

After each of the following petitions, all respond, "Hear our prayer, O Lord."

For school boards and superintendents,

For principals and secretaries,

For custodians and bus drivers,

For librarians and cooks,

For teachers and learners,

For buildings and playgrounds,

For budgets and books,

For parents and families,

For assignments and grades,

For programs and games,

For field days and field trips,

For book reports and homework,

For kindergartners and school aides,

For first graders and reading teachers,

For second graders and music teachers,

For third graders and school nurses,

For fourth graders and room mothers,

For fifth graders and speech therapists,

For sixth graders and playground supervisors,

For seventh graders and assistant principals,

For eighth graders and resource people,

For freshmen and activity directors,

For sophomores and coaches,

For juniors and drama directors,

For seniors and counselors,

Keep us all under your loving eye this year, Lord,

and teach us to love one another
as we learn from each other.

After each of the following petitions, all respond, "Pray for us."

Mary, mother of all students,
That we may learn to be what God wants us to be,
That we may accept the responsibilities of learning,
That we may support our schools and teachers,
That we may perceive, judge, and act wisely,
That we may grow in age and grace,
That we may furnish educational hope for all,
That we may change the world,
That we may make new friends and keep old friends,
That we may be patient with our students
    and with our teachers,
That we may keep our school clean and pleasant,
Come, O Holy Spirit, and fill the hearts and minds of your faithful. Grant us faith, knowledge, and perseverance so that we may go forth and spread the Good News. Amen.

Prayer for a Dropout

Dear God, I am so weary today. My son dropped out of school. I am a failure. What did I do wrong? I went to PTA; I checked his homework—all the right things. What did I do wrong?

Sometimes I think it would be easier not to be a parent, God. All those grades, all those truancies, and now this. For what? What can he do in life? Work in a gas station? Drive a truck? Yes, I know somebody has to drive a truck but why him? He has so much potential.

What is your plan for him? Help me to understand, please. I feel so alone and such a failure. Help him to find his way and help me to accept it. Thank you, God.

The Student's ABCs

Appreciate the sound of silence.

Books are meant to be opened, not carried.

Christmas vacation will come.

Doing the right thing is hard, but right.

Everybody is smart on some topic.

Four-letter words belong in the bathroom.

God will help, but you have to ask.

Helping others makes you feel good.

"I can't do it," means, "I won't try."

Just getting by means, "I'm not worth it."

Keeping a friend beats always being right.

Long boring classes will end.

Mom and Dad went to school, too.

"No" means "no," not "maybe."

Outside days are God's little rewards.

Putting off homework makes it harder.

Questions are never dumb.

Recess is your coffee break. Enjoy it.

School is fun only if you decide to like it.

Television is not life.

Until you like yourself, nobody else can.

Very little breakfast means yawns at ten.

Watching the clock slows it down.

X-ray eyes are given to mothers and teachers.

You are lovable and capable. Believe it.

Zilch is what you get if zilch if what you do.

A Parent's Prayer for the Teacher

O Mary, mother of the greatest of teachers,
    fill my child's teacher with patience and understanding.
Help her to understand that he tries,
    even if he doesn't always achieve.
I know that she has a class full of students,

but if you could let her know that his stoniness
    covers his humiliation at times,
or that his awkwardness
    comes from trying too hard to please,
or that his exaggerations
    stem from a need to be recognized,
he and I will be forever grateful.
Let me be more patient and understanding
    of my child's teacher, too.
Teach me to look at both sides of an issue
    before I take my child's word.
Help me to reassure the teacher
    that she is loved and appreciated.
And let me offer to help her
    when she needs a paper-corrector or a cupcake-maker,
    or just a friend who happens to be a parent.

School Program Time

Dear God, let him remember his lines.
Help her reach the high notes.
Don't let him trip,
    or stand mute,
    or cry—
Please!

A Girl's Prayer to Teresa of Avila

St. Teresa, you never pretended to be less bright than you really were; help me today. Invite me to consider you as model, O Doctor of the Church.

Help me rid myself of that obsolete notion that smart girls must play dumb. Let me be proud of my scholarship, not embarrassed. Help me know that the boys and men who count are more interested in my mind than in my hair.

A Parent's Prayer at Report Card Time

O God, who sent us children of such different talents,
    help us to appreciate them for what they are.
Help us not to overpraise the scholar
    and underpraise the dreamer.
Inspire us, as parents, to say the right words
    to let them all know they are loved equally,
    no matter what their grades.
And thank you, God,
    for not grading parents.

School Dance (Version 1)

Jesus, I want to go to the dance.
But I'm afraid to ask a girl.
What if she says no? What will I say?
What will the guys say?
Why would she want to go with me?
Help me not to be so scared, Jesus.
She's just a girl...
Just a girl??!! (like I ask one everyday).
Let her say yes, Jesus.
Please let her say yes.

School Dance (Version 2)

Jesus, I want to go to the dance.
But what boy will ask me?
Why would he want to go with me?
My hair is brown. I'm not exactly skinny.
And I'm not a cheerleader.
Still, Jesus, I want to go to the dance.
Let someone ask me.
Please, Jesus. Please.

School Dance (Version 3)

They're off to the dance, Jesus.

Thank you for their dates.

They're so excited, so awkward, so adolescent
   on the threshold of maturity.

Help us to let them go, Jesus.

Part of me thrills at their growing-up;
   but part rebels.

They are such children.

How can they go to a long-dress dance
   when they can't even find their sneakers?

Anyway, let them have a good time tonight.

Keep them out of high-speed cars on icy highways,
   and out of dark cars on dead-end roads.

Help them to handle any situation that might arise.

Keep them in the palm of your hand, dear Jesus,
   and help their parents realize
   that they are growing up
   to become their own persons.

PRAYERS FOR SPECIAL DAYS

House Blessing

Bless our home, and make it fit for you, O God.

Send your Holy Spirit into each nook and cranny.

Let the walls resound with love and laughter.

Let your birds sing on your trees outside
   and your lilies flourish in the garden.

Bless our kitchen
   and fill it with the warmth of shared bread.

Bless our family room
   and fill it with loving communication.

Bless our bedrooms
   and fill them with restful slumber.

Bless each room and each of us, dear God,
and make yourself at home with us.

A Birthday Prayer

For (*child's name*) who is (*age*) today,
thank you, Lord.
Just as a finger is part of a hand,
he/she is part of all of us, of our family.
Help him/her to have a good birthday
with lots of love and happiness.
Let him/her have a good year
and let us all be together again in good health
on this day next year
to help him/her celebrate being (*age next year*).

A First Eucharist Prayer

Bless (child's name), Jesus,
and invite him/her to be a regular guest at your table.
By the sharing of your bread and wine,
help him/her to share your life in others.
O Lord of the loaves and fishes,
who nourishes us all with your body and blood
and your spirit, let us rejoice.
May his/her new life in you
bring us ever closer together.

A First Penance Prayer

For your forgiveness, we thank you, Lord.
For your loving reconciliation, we bless you, Lord.
For our new penitent, we pray to you, Lord.
For your gift of this sacrament, we praise you, Lord.

Lord, come into the depths of our souls and help us as a family to appreciate always the wonder of your forgiveness and to regularly receive the sacrament of reconciliation. Bless our child whose first penance is soon to take place. Erase his/her fears and fill him/her with the hope of your forgiving love.

A Confirmation Prayer

Come, O Holy Spirit, and fill the heart of (*child's name*). Make him/her strong in purpose, pure in heart, and always Christian in motive.

Thank you for (*name*), whom you blessed in baptism, blessed again in first eucharist and first penance, and now bless in confirmation. Fill all your people with joy, love, and your beloved Spirit.

On the Death of a Grandparent

We have lost a dear parent and grandparent, Lord. Be with us in our grief.

Let us remember both the life on earth he/she shared with us and the eternal happiness he/she now shares with you. You taught us that anyone who believes in you will have eternal life. Help us to remember that when little memories triggering our grief tug at us each day.

Thank you for this parent and grandparent, Lord—for the years of love and care, for the memories we shared, and for the hope you offer us.

First Funeral

Muffled voices
   silver box
   sacred sounds
   sweet scents.

Words...
> tears...
Why?
Yes, child,
> people die.
Why?
Sheltered from age,
> surrounded by youth,
> you wonder...
God, can it be true
> that someday
> I...?

Winning and Losing

Here she comes, Lord, and her disappointed face tells it all. She lost. Help me to find the right words to console her, to explain that in order to experience winning, we must also experience losing. Otherwise, how flat life's victories!

But when is it ever a good time to lose? Last time or next time, maybe, but never now. Should I remind her that she won the spelling bee in second grade? Or that she brought home four blue ribbons from fourth grade field day? Or that she was elected seventh grade senator? No, what good will that serve now? Later, perhaps. Now she needs to be consoled. Help me to help her save face, Lord, while learning to accept wins and losses.

And while I'm at it, Lord, help me to accept losing, too. It hurts to see my children disappointed. Help me to realize that when my child loses, another child wins and that child deserves the joy of victory also.

Illness in the Family

Dearest Jesus, come into our family and make us well

again. When one is ill, the rest of us also hurt. Grant wisdom to our doctors and nurses, patience to ourselves, and relief to our sick member. You who healed the many while you walked on earth will not refuse to hear our prayer today.

Graduation

Bless our graduate, Lord, and thank you for his/her education. Through the teachers, talents, and perseverance you sent, he/she has gained knowledge to face the future with hope.

We pray that our graduate will use this education to your greater honor and glory, Lord, never forgetting responsibility to those less learned. And we also pray that we will all continue to be lifelong learners.

For Children Going Away to College

Seek not grades but understanding.
Seek not popularity but friends.
Seek not promotion but fulfillment.
Seek not success but service.
Seek not pleasure but joy.
Seek not affluence but peace.
Seek not compromise but truth.
Seek not attention but respect.
Seek not yourself but others.
Seek not heaven but God.

An Engagement Prayer

Come into our home, blessed Mother Mary, and share the joy of our engaged couple. Let their love radiate in our midst, engulfing us and renewing in us the joy of having others love us.

Just as our Lord blessed you in your betrothal, bless our betrothed ones. Fill them with hope and let Christ become an integral part of their new life together.

Wedding Anniversary

We praise and thank you for our years together
    for the joys and the sorrows,
    for the lean years and the full years,
    for the sons and the daughters
    and for everything else.
We praise and thank you
    for bringing us together
    and for enriching that togetherness
    through you and in you and with you,
    O Father, Son, and Holy Spirit.

Renewal of Wedding Vows

Husband: I, (*husband's name*), again take you, (*wife's name*), to be my wedded wife, to have and to hold from this day forward, for better or for worse, for richer or for poorer, in sickness and in health, until death do us part.

OR:

I, (*husband's name*), again take you, (*wife's name*), to be my wife. I promise to be true to you in good times and in bad, in sickness and in health. I will love you and honor you all the days of my life.

Wife: I, (*wife's name*), again take you, (*husband's name*), to be my wedded husband, to have and to hold from this day forward, for better or for worse, for richer or for poorer, in sickness and in health, until death do us part.

OR:

> I, (*wife's name*), again take you, (*husband's name*), to be my husband. I promise to be true to you in good times and in bad, in sickness and in health. I will love you and honor you all the days of my life.

Together: May God continue to unite us in ever richer love and strengthen us for our lives ahead. May he fill our hearts with joy and our home with love. May he constantly remind us of his great gift of one another. May his blessings be upon our family forever.

Safe Travel

O good St. Joseph, patron saint of travelers,
    watch over our loved ones as they travel.
Grant them safe planes, careful pilots, and good weather.
Give them clear highways,
    reasonable speeds, and concern for other drivers.
Just as you guided Jesus and Mary safely back to Nazareth,
    return our loved ones to us safely.

Vacation Prayer in the Car With Tired Children

O God of Peace,
    invade our car
    and turn it into a haven of peace and quiet
    for just a little while.
Give the children a little patience with one another
    and us a lot more patience with them.
In the miles to go before we stop,
    help them realize their power
    to make each other happy or unhappy.

Make them willing to share the windows,
   to stop touching each other,
   to stop asking when we'll get there.
Finally, dear Lord, teach us to appreciate
   the luxury of auto travel today.
We could be traveling steerage across the Atlantic
   or in a covered wagon across the Rockies.
Alongside such hazards,
   the kids' fighting seems insignificant.
Help us to hold our tempers for just a few more miles.

Halloween Prayer
Mother Mary, hallowed of hallowed,
   come to my aid this hallowed season.
Give me inspiration, patience, and Elmer's glue
   to create something different for my human goblins.
Guide my needle true and I pray, dear Mother,
   that you help me find time—
   between this, that, and the other thing—
   to watch for tricks and buy the treats
   and ponder once again
   how this holiday came about.

Thanksgiving
We thank you, O Lord God, giver of all fruits of the earth,
   for your bounteous gifts:
   land, home, sustenance, and universe.
We thank you, O Lord God, creator of all that lives,
   for your loving gifts:
   families, friends, communities, peoples.
We thank you, O Lord God, promiser of eternal life,
   for your glorious gifts:
   your love, your Son, and your Holy Spirit.

RECORDING
SACRAMENTAL
MILESTONES

In times past, the family Bible carefully recorded the sacramental life of the family from weddings and baptisms to funerals. Many families have drifted away from this beautiful custom and legacy to future generations either out of neglect or unawareness, or perhaps lack of a place in which to record significant sacramental moments.

We record that which is important to us. Many families have a more accurate record of their children's immunizations than of their baptisms, first eucharists, and confirmations. To encourage readers to return to the meaningful practice of recording sacramental milestones, I offer these pages and invite you to use them as a record for future generations. Or use them as a model for your own family Book of Life, one that may exist as its own entity or as part of a treasured family Bible or album.

Dear God,
hold this family
in the cup of your hand.
Watch over us with a loving eye.
Keep us on your path
so that someday
we may be joined together again
with you in heaven. Amen.

OUR FAMILY BEGINS

We,_____

and_____

freely chose one another in love

and were married in God's grace

at _____ o'clock

on the_____ day of_____

in the year_____

at _____ Church

in the city of_____.

Here follows a record of our life together.

BIRTHS

Name_____

Date_____Time_____

Place_____

Name_____

Date_____Time_____

Place_____

Name_____

Date_____Time_____

Place_____

Name_____

Date_____Time_____

Place_____

Name_____

Date_____Time_____

Place_____

Name_____

Date_____Time_____

Place_____

Name_____

Date_____Time_____

Place_____

BAPTISMS

Name_____
Parish_____
Godparents_____
_____ Date_____

Name_____
Parish_____
Godparents_____
_____ Date_____

Name_____
Parish_____
Godparents_____
_____ Date_____

Name_____
Parish_____
Godparents_____
_____ Date_____

Name_____
Parish_____
Godparents_____
_____ Date_____

Name_____
Parish_____
Godparents_____
_____ Date_____

PATRON SAINTS

Name_____

Feast_____

Patron_____

Name_____

Feast_____

Patron_____

Name_____

Feast_____

Patron_____

Name_____

Feast_____

Patron_____

Name_____

Feast_____

Patron_____

Name_____

Feast_____

Patron_____

Name_____

Feast_____

Patron_____

FIRST EUCHARIST

Name_____

Parish_____

Celebrant_____Date_____

Name_____

Parish_____

Celebrant_____Date_____

Name_____

Parish_____

Celebrant_____Date_____

Name_____

Parish_____

Celebrant_____Date_____

Name_____

Parish_____

Celebrant_____Date_____

Name_____

Parish_____

Celebrant_____Date_____

Name_____

Parish_____

Celebrant_____Date_____

CONFIRMATIONS

Name_____
Parish_____Date_____
Sponsor_____
Bishop _____

Name_____
Parish_____Date_____
Sponsor_____
Bishop _____

Name_____
Parish_____Date_____
Sponsor_____
Bishop _____

Name_____
Parish_____Date_____
Sponsor_____
Bishop _____

Name_____
Parish_____Date_____
Sponsor_____
Bishop _____

Name_____
Parish_____Date_____
Sponsor_____
Bishop _____

MARRIAGES

Bride _____

Groom _____

Place _____

Celebrant_____Date_____

Witnesses_____

_____

Bride _____

Groom _____

Place _____

Celebrant_____Date_____

Witnesses_____

_____

Bride _____

Groom _____

Place _____

Celebrant_____Date_____

Witnesses_____

_____

Bride _____

Groom _____

Place _____

Celebrant_____Date_____

Witnesses_____

_____

Bride _____

Groom _____

Place _____

Celebrant_____Date_____

Witnesses_____

_____

Bride _____

Groom _____

Place _____

Celebrant_____Date_____

Witnesses_____

_____

Bride _____

Groom _____

Place _____

Celebrant_____Date_____

Witnesses_____

_____

Bride _____

Groom _____

Place _____

Celebrant_____Date_____

Witnesses_____

_____

ORDINATIONS

Name_____

Place _____Date_____

Bishop_____

Name_____

Place _____Date_____

Bishop_____

Name_____

Place _____Date_____

Bishop_____

RELIGIOUS PROFESSIONS

Name_____

Community _____

Date of First Profession_____

Date of Final Vows_____

Name_____

Community _____

Date of First Profession_____

Date of Final Vows_____

Name_____

Community _____

Date of First Profession_____

Date of Final Vows_____

DEATHS

Name_____Date_____
Cemetery_____Age_____

Name_____Date_____
Cemetery_____Age_____

Name_____Date_____
Cemetery_____Age_____

Name_____Date_____
Cemetery_____Age_____

Name_____Date_____
Cemetery_____Age_____

Name_____Date_____
Cemetery_____Age_____

Name_____Date_____
Cemetery_____Age_____

Name_____Date_____
Cemetery_____Age_____

Name_____Date_____
Cemetery_____Age_____

MISCELLANEOUS

SUGGESTED RESOURCES

BOOKS

Calderone-Stewart, Lisa-Marie. *In Touch with the Word: Lectionary Based Prayer Reflections: Advent, Christmas, Lent, and Easter.* Winona, MN: St. Mary's Press.

Chesto, Kathleen O'Connell. *Family Prayer for Family Times: Traditions, Celebrations, and Ritual.* Mystic, CT: Twenty-Third Publications.

Edelman, Marian Wright. *Guide My Feet: Prayers and Meditations on Loving and Working for Children.* Boston, MA: Beacon Press.

Faith and Fest in Family: A Collection of Prayers and Celebration Resources Linking Parish and Home. Omaha, NE: Catholic Archdiocese of Omaha.

Finley, Kathleen. *Dear God: Prayers for Families With Children.* Mystic, CT: Twenty-Third Publications.

Hunt, Jeanne. *Holy Bells and Wonderful Smells: Year-Round Activities for Classrooms and Families.* Cincinnati, OH: St. Anthony Messenger Press.

Jones, Susan. *The Way of the Cross for Parents.* Mystic, CT: Twenty-Third Publications.

Kielly, Shiela, and Geraghty, Sheila. *Camels, Carols, Crosses, Crowns: Advent and Lent Activities for Children.* Mystic, CT: Twenty-Third Publications.

McGinnis, James, Park, Mary Joan and Jerry, and others. *Families Caring: At Home, In the Community, For the Earth: Practical Ideas for Families and Intergenerational Programs.* St. Louis, MO: The Parenting for Peace and Justice Network.

Meehan, Bridget Mary. *Prayers, Activities, Celebrations (and More) for Catholic Families.* Mystic, CT: Twenty-Third Publications.

Peace Begins at Home: Rituals and Resources for Peacemaking Pittsburgh, PA: Pax Christi USA.

Plueddemann, Carl and Wright, Vinita Hampton. *Prayers Around the Family Table.* Wheaton, IL: Harold Shaw Publishers.

Thomas, David M. and Calnan, Mary Joyce. *The Catechism of the Catholic Church: Familystyle.* Allen, TX: Tabor Publishing Company.

Travnikar, Rock, OFM. *The Blessing Cup: 40 Simple Rites for Family Prayer-Celebrations.* Cincinnati, OH: St. Anthony Messenger Press.

When Someone Dies: Children's Grief Workbook. Mystic, CT: Twenty-Third Publications.

NEWSLETTERS

Bringing Religion Home - a monthly newsletter from Claretian Publications; 205 N. Monroe St., Chicago, IL 60606.

Growing Faith, Growing Family - a monthly publication from Twenty-Third Publications, 185 Willow St., Mystic, CT, 06355.

Our Family - a seasonal (liturgical) newsletter from Treehaus Communications; P.O. Box 249, Loveland, OH 45140-0249.

Parenting for Peace and Justice - a bimonthly newsletter from the Institute for Peace and Justice; 4144 Lindell Blvd., # 124, St. Louis, MO 63108.

VIDEOS

The following publishers offer video programs that are great for family use. Write for a catalog, or ask your pastor or DRE for help in locating more information on what's available.

Center for Ministry Development, P.O. Box 699, Naugatuck, CT 06770

Our Sunday Visitor, 200 Noll Plaza, Huntington, IN 46750

Pauline Books and Media, 50 St. Paul's Ave., Boston, MA 02130

Paulist Press, 997 Macarthur Blvd., Mahwah, NJ 07430

Tabor Publishing, P.O. Box 7000, Allen, TX 75002

Twenty-Third Publications, 185 Willow Street, Mystic, CT 06355

Videos with Values, 1944 Innerbelt Bus. Ctr. Dr., St. Louis, MO 63114-5718

MUSIC

These publishers all offer hymnals and choral collections that are useful in the home.

GIA Publications, 7404 S. Mason Ave., Chicago, IL 60638

Hope Publishing Company, 380 S. Main Pl., Carol Stream, IL 60188

Oregon Catholic Press, 5536 NE Hassalo, Portland, OR 97213

INDEX